fragrant GARDENING

Steve & Val Bradley

with photography by Andrea Jones

LAUREL
GLEN

San Diego, California

CONTENTS

1
The search for scent

2
Designing a fragrant garden

3
The fragrant garden in spring

fragrant GARDENING

CONTENTS

4
The fragrant garden in summer

5
The fragrant garden in fall

6
The fragrant garden in winter

introduction

Scent is the oxidization of essential oils found in the flowers and leaves of plants, but it is more than a simple chemical process. The fragrance of a flower or the aroma of a leaf lifts the spirits and warms the heart. From roses and honeysuckle growing around a secluded seat in high summer to wintersweet and winter jasmine flowering near a doorway during the coldest months, there is an endless variety of plants that can perfume your garden throughout the seasons.

Types of scent

Scented plants give life to the garden and make simply being there a pleasant experience. However, just as plants vary greatly in terms of color and size of bloom, they also differ in fragrance. The scent of some plants is bold and intense, while the scent of others is more delicate and subtle—the choice is at the discretion of the gardener. For example, if you prefer floral fragrances, you could choose the intoxicating aroma of hyacinths (*Hyacinthus*) or the sweet scent of lily of the valley (*Convallaria majalis*). However, if you prefer fresh, herby scents, you could choose the pinelike aroma of rosemary (*Rosmarinus officinalis*) or the stimulating fragrance of chives (*Allium schoenoprasum*).

Outdoor living

These days, outdoor living is becoming more a part of our lives, in part because houses are becoming smaller and the weather warmer. Where gardens were once considered ornamental or productive, we now expect much more from them. They are still for sitting and relaxing in, but also for playing, entertaining, and dining, and there is no reason why even a small garden cannot accommodate these aspects as well as a host of delightful

fragrances. In a large garden, you may choose to place a scented plant so that it becomes a focal point and draws attention by its sheer presence. In a small area or on a patio, you can grow the plant in a container and move it to wherever it will be closest to you, in order to appreciate its beauty. This might be near a door that you use frequently, under a regularly opened window, or adjacent to the dining area so that you can enjoy the fragrance while entertaining friends.

Attracting wildlife

Fragrant plants attract insects to the garden, and if you want to create a wildlife-friendly garden, you can even use a specific scent to encourage a particular species. Bees and butterflies prefer sweet scents such as lavender (*Lavandula*); moths are attracted to flowers that are fragrant during the evening, such as night-scented stock (*Matthiola longipetala*); beetles like the fruity scents of plants like lemon balm (*Melissa officinalis*); and flies prefer fetid smells such as purple trillium (*Trillium erectum*). Birds are attracted by color rather than fragrance, but you can combine the two by planting crimson and gold varieties of scented flowers such as primrose (*Primula*) and crocus (*Crocus*).

Uses of scent

Scent is not just an attractive feature for the garden. Scented plants can also be used in the home in a variety of ways, and the flowers and leaves do not even have to be fresh to be of benefit. The essential oils of many fragrant plants are used in aromatherapy because their healing properties are recognized as aids to the body and spirit. Dried flowers can be used in potpourri, lavender bags, and pillows to aid relaxation, scent the atmosphere, and keep moths away from clothes in a closet. The dry bark of eucalyptus (*Eucalyptus*) gives potpourri a refreshing aroma, and the leaves of herbs can be dried and stored for use in cooking and medicinal preparations, even when the plants themselves are dormant. Bunches of herbs hung in the kitchen can repel flies in summer, and leaves thrown on the barbecue while you cook can deter biting insects.

Planning your garden

The aim of this book is to show you how, with a little planning and preparation, your garden can be a source of fragrance throughout the year. The first chapter examines the history of

Plants such as this milkweed (Asclepias) will fill your garden with summer fragrance as well as attract pollinating insects.

scented plants and explains how scents are classified. It then looks at the many ways in which essential oils can be used, as well as how to harvest and dry the different parts of plants. The second chapter guides you through the basic principles of garden design, enabling you to make the most of fragrance no matter the size of the area you are dealing with.

Season by season

The remainder of the book is divided into four chapters, one for each season of the year. Each chapter contains information about fragrant plants for the season in question and explains the jobs you may need to do in the garden at that time of year. There is also advice on the selection, cultivation, and propagation of a wide range of plants. In addition, each seasonal chapter features several projects, with clearly photographed steps, to help you achieve some wonderful effects with fragrance in your

This garden design has used a mixed planting scheme to create a pretty pond area surrounded by fragrant and colorful flowers.

garden. These range from basic techniques, such as propagating a fragrant plant, to more elaborate undertakings, such as creating a scented walkway.

Plant directories

At the end of each seasonal chapter, you will find a plant directory that describes some of the fragrant plants that flourish at that time of year, from trees and shrubs to perennials and annuals, and with scents ranging from fruit to honey and cloves to violets. For each plant there is a photograph, a description of its physical characteristics and fragrance, as well as advice on pruning and propagation.

THE SEARCH FOR SCENT THE SEARCH FOR SCENT THE SEARCH THE SEARCH FOR SCENT... FOR SCENT THE SEARCH FOR SCENT

chapter one

1

A fragrant history

The use of scent dates back to the earliest civilizations and has played a role in food preservation, medicine, and human ritual ever since. Spices and gums such as cinnamon and frankincense have been popular preservatives for millennia. In the sun-baked, arid area known today as the Middle East—one of the main centers of early civilization—trees were highly valued. Their leaves provided much-needed shade for people and animals, and the volatile oils given off in the heat were so refreshing that branches were cut and placed indoors. The use of perfumed oils dates back to the ancient Egyptians, who distilled parts of flowers and plants for application to their bodies both in life and death. The word "perfume" itself derives from the Latin *per*, meaning "through," and *fumum*, meaning "smoke," denoting its early value as incense.

The Garden of Eden

Written 4,000 years before the birth of Christ, the Bible's book of Genesis describes how the Garden of Eden was created by God as an earthly paradise. Research suggests that the garden was located between the Tigris and Euphrates rivers, in an area known as Babylonia. The river that irrigated the garden flowed on to the land of Havilah, where gold, onyx, and bdellium were found. Bdellium is possibly the prickly shrub *Commiphora myrrha*, from which the aromatic resinous gum myrrh is obtained. In the days before alcohol was developed as a means of dissolving the essential oils of flowers, myrrh was much prized for its strong and long-lasting fragrance.

The spice trade

Trading in spices and aromatics—the scented leaves and bark of plants, dried or distilled—began around 2000 B.C. with the Egyptians, and caravan routes quickly developed around Egypt, Arabia, and Palestine. The most commonly traded substances were myrrh, spices, and a balm that was extracted from trees and used for burning as incense, chewing, or, later, for flavoring drinks by the Greeks. Jericho was a major trading point for local goods such as cedarwood, believed by the Egyptians to last forever. It was much sought after for use in coffins and as cedarwood oil, one of the most expensive body oils. Aromatic spikenard (*Nardostachys jatamansi*) was brought from the Himalayas, and Arabia yielded the fragrant gum frankincense, prized second only to myrrh.

As civilization spread, more plants were discovered and trade expanded. Egypt traded copper and turquoise for sandalwood trees (*Santalum album*) and various incense trees. Plant products such as saffron, aloe, cinnamon, and ginger became desirable commodities, and flowers were also highly prized, including lilies (*Lilium*), lotus (*Nelumbo*), and water lilies (*Nymphaea*). Roots were perhaps the most valuable part of a plant because they could be dried and stored. One of the oldest recorded plants, *Iris germanica florentina*, has strongly violet-scented roots, and the intensity increases as the roots wither, until they eventually give off a stronger scent than violets themselves. Ground into the powder known as orrisroot, they were used whenever fragrance was desired.

Common evening primrose (Oenothera biennis) *has long been prized for its medicinal benefts as well as its sweet fragrance. The oil obtained from its seeds is considered to be particularly therapeutic.*

Many scented plants were also spread from country to country by invaders. The Romans, for example, introduced ginger (*Zingiber officinale*) to the colder climates of northern Europe, growing it on a hotbed system over composting material. They were also responsible for spreading many herbs, including chives (*Allium schoenoprasum*), rosemary (*Rosmarinus*), sage (*Salvia officinalis*), and thyme (*Thymus*), from their warm Mediterranean habitats to the northerly outposts of the Roman Empire.

Early use of fragrance

The Greeks used fragrant oils to ward off illness, sprinkled furnishings with scented water, and placed garlands of fragrant flowers around the necks of their guests. They also used perfumes and flowers in funeral rites. The Greek philosopher and scientist Theophrastus (c. 370–287 B.C.) wrote an early study of perfumes entitled *Concerning Odors*. He described how a poultice on the leg could sweeten the breath by the essences permeating the skin and entering the circulatory system.

The Romans adopted many Greek uses for perfumes. Saffron crocus (*Crocus sativus*) was highly prized and used in cooking, as a dye, and in oils. Saffron is the dried stigma of the autumn crocus, which ripens only in hot, dry weather. It has more commercial uses than almost any other plant, but it is expensive, as 70,000 blooms are needed to produce just one pound of saffron. The Romans liked to prove their wealth by strewing saffron on the floors of their villas.

Roses (*Rosa*), hyacinths (*Hyacinthus*), myrtle (*Myrtus*), and jonquil (*Narcissus jonquilla*) were popular in seventh-century Eastern civilizations, where the wealthy surrounded themselves with plants that were aromatic or produced strongly fragrant flowers. Musk was the most popular fragrance, and the followers of Mohammed mixed it with mortar when building their places of worship, to give lasting fragrance. The Koran mentions that the floor of the Garden of Paradise is covered with wheat flour mixed with musk and saffron. Musk-scented roses grew throughout Syria, and their use is traditional as oils and unguents, and as petals either strewn or floating in bowls of water.

Many Hindu ceremonies use fragrant woods, flowers, and perfumes. In India, roses (*Rosa*) and jasmine (*Jasminum*) are used to make perfumed oil. Traditional Indian medicine, Ayurveda, uses essential oils and dates back to 1000 B.C. In China, jasmine flowers are used to make fragrant tea. Fragrant flowers are also hung in houses and temples on festive occasions.

Scent in medieval times

In medieval Europe, flowers were used to decorate churches on festive days. They were cultivated in monastery gardens along with the herbs used for medicinal and culinary purposes. The packed-earth floors and small windows of the times also meant that buildings and churches smelled musty, so fragrant seasonal flowers, herbs, and sweet-smelling grasses and rushes were strewn on the pews and floors. The scented sweet flag (*Acorus calamus*) had numerous uses in addition to strewing. It also yielded a volatile oil from the leaves, and the root could be used to flavor beer and wine, or could be dried and powdered for use as talcum powder. Herbs were particularly useful for strewing because they released a fragrance when walked upon. For many years, royal households had an official "Strewer of Herbs."

Other plants were used for their repellent abilities rather than for their fragrances. Green rushes strewn on floors could attract fleas and other insects, so it was customary to burn repellents such as pungent fleabane (*Erigeron acris*) to avoid infestation. Common rue (*Ruta graveolens*) was used in the sickroom to drive away disease-carrying bugs.

From Renaissance to present day

Pomanders were another popular ward against disease, and Elizabethan pomanders consisted of a dried orange or lemon studded with cloves, or a container with a sponge soaked in scented vinegar. Later, silver pomanders were made, based on the orange, with filigree segments hinged at the base and held by a clasp at the top, each of which could hold a separate perfume.

In the sixteenth century, sprinkling scented water on furnishings and fabrics became fashionable throughout Europe. Flowers and leaves were distilled in the large houses of the wealthy for personal use, cooking, and as medicine. The kitchen garden would provide rose petals and numerous herbs that could be used fresh or dried. Clothes and linens were stored in chests made from fragrant wood, such as sandalwood, cedar, or juniper, so that the scent would permeate the fabric.

Cloves, orris powder, lemon, and oils of thyme and spikenard could be used to make perfumed waters or a dry potpourri to add fragrance to a room. Itinerant salesmen would sell cheap substitutes such as roseroot (*Sedum rhodiola*, now *Rhodiola rosea*)—which grew freely on walls and cliffs and smelled of rose when the root was crushed—and beads of hardened gum molded using hands dipped in jasmine oil so that the scent was absorbed.

Both the Greeks and Romans had used powdered root as talcum powder, and it was also widely used in Elizabethan times. The powder might be inserted in a sachet and used to perfume linen, dusted onto a lady's hair, or blended as snuff. Linen sachets would contain orrisroot or the powdered roots of herbs. Many dried leaves were powdered and used in snuff, which was taken to clear the head of a cold and improve the temperament. At the time of Shakespeare, combinations of orrisroot and Roman chamomile (*Chamaemelum nobile*) were popular.

Perfumes also came into general use during this time, when exotic new fragrances were brought back from the New World and other far-flung locations. Queen Elizabeth I, for example, was given a pair of scented Italian gloves, probably perfumed with frangipani. Similar to jasmine, frangipani is distilled from the flowers of *Plumeria*, a sweet-smelling flower found in Antigua, Jamaica, and Martinique.

Contemporary fragrance

Scented flowers and aromatic gardening fell into decline during the eighteenth century, when landscape gardening, with its emphasis on dramatic vistas rather than floral displays, became popular. The Victorians remedied this to some extent with their love of flower beds, although they tended to concentrate on color rather than fragrance. By the turn of the twentieth century, however, the aromatic garden had begun to rise again in popularity and, in more recent times, there has been a strong revival of interest in both aromatherapy—the use of aromatic plant extracts and essential oils for healing and cosmetic purposes—and gardening. Fueled to a large extent by the need to relax from the stresses of modern life, the garden is seen as the perfect haven, filled with a healing blend of fragrant plants.

Commercially, the interest in aromatic plants has never been more intense. Perfume is a huge industry, and many Hollywood celebrities vie with one another to name a best-selling fragrance. The town of Grasse in southern France is one of the world's largest centers for the production and development of fragrances, and it devotes many of its financial resources to intensive plant-breeding programs designed to produce varieties with greater concentrations of sought-after essential oils.

Dried leaves, flowers, berries, spices, peel, and bark were used to make potpourri in the sixteenth century. Often enhanced with essential oils, the mixture helped to perfume the home and mask unwanted smells.

Classification of scent

Scent appeals to the olfactory senses just as music appeals to the ear. There is a range of odors in the same way that there is a scale of notes, and a perfume needs to have its notes in harmony or there will be discord. Certain odors blend naturally together, such as almond, vanilla, and heliotrope, or patchouli, cedar, and sandalwood. On a higher "octave" come verbena and citron, and even higher comes the combination of rose and neroli (orange blossom derived from the Seville orange, *Citrus aurantium*). Combinations such as these occur throughout the plant kingdom, and it is said that the perfumer has 4,000 raw materials from which to work with—the finished perfume can be likened to the creation of a symphony.

Reactions to scent

The sense of smell is the most basic of human senses. Scents are detected by tiny filaments at the top of the nose, where olfactory cells connect directly into the central nervous system. Too much perfume overpowers these sensitive nerve endings and reduces one's ability to appreciate the scent. Different people also respond in different ways to scent, with dark-haired people having a keener sense of smell than fair-haired ones, making perfumes notoriously difficult to categorize.

Some scents are best enjoyed from a distance, because they change when they are too concentrated. For example, the aroma of Austrian briar rose (*Rosa foetida*) is pleasant from afar, but get too close and the smell becomes that of rotten fish because of the presence of indole (a natural plant chemical that is also present in rotting animal tissue). Indole is also responsible for the cloying sweetness of flowers such as lily (*Lilium*) and jonquil (*Narcissus jonquilla*). Another plant chemical, aminoides, is found in white or off-white flowers and can make them smell of ammonia and attract flies.

The fragrances of some plants, such as hyacinths (*Hyacinthus*), tire the olfactory nerves so that, from being initially attractive, the scent becomes less pleasant and, in the case of violets, changes to the smell of cut cucumber or damp moss. The fragrance of leaves is seldom as oppressive as that of flowers because of the presence of different chemicals, such as geraniol, which is found in the rose-scented geranium (*Pelargonium capitatum*).

The reaction to scent is not purely a question of aesthetics. Perfumes also have a definite effect on health. Violets (*Viola*), for example, have rendered singers unable to produce a note by affecting their vocal chords. Beans and night-scented stock (*Matthiola longipetala*) have an intoxicating effect, and the common gorse (*Ulex europaeus*) is reputed to cure headaches with its fresh, fruity scent.

Constituents of scent

Fragrance is not composed of a single substance, but is actually a composite of chemicals exuded by different parts of the plant. The most pure—and difficult to imitate—is the essential oil generally found on the upper side of the petals or sepals of the

The flowers of the lemon (Citrus limon) are classified in the Lemon group of scents. They have the same tangy fragrance as the fruit.

flowers. As the plant develops, the cells of the flower (which at first contain only chlorophyll) change to hold other substances, such as tannin or the essential oil. The oil is stored with sugars as a glycoside in cells from which the protoplasm (original cell contents) has been removed. The fragrance is released as the glycoside decays, a process that slows or stops at certain times of day or if the flower closes again. Some oils are more volatile than others, with those having a low degree of volatility (such as patchouli and cedar) being classed as stronger than those with a high degree of volatility (such as lavender).

Flower perfume groups

Although the scents of flowers are wide-ranging, there are several clearly identified perfume groups. However, since some flowers fall between groups and identification tends to be personal, these cannot be exactly quantified.

- **Heavy group**
  Strong, lasting scents and flowers that are often white or cream in color, such as *Lilium candidum*, *Philadelphus*, lilac (*Syringa*), and lily of the valley (*Convallaria majalis*).

- **Aromatic group**
  Pleasant fragrances of cinnamon, clove, vanilla, and balsam, including pinks and carnations (*Dianthus*), *Viburnum carlesii*, hyacinths (*Hyachinthus*), and night-scented stock (*Matthiola longipetala*).

- **Violet group**
  A sweet scent that can tire the senses, such as *Iris reticulata*, *Acacia*, and garden mignonette (*Reseda odorata*).

- **Rose group**
  A light, sweetly fruity fragrance, including rose-scented geranium (*Pelargonium capitatum*).

- **Lemon group**
  A refreshing, tangy fragrance, such as *Rosa bracteata*, *Oenothera odorata*, and *Nymphaea odorata*.

- **Fruit-scented group**
  A wide-ranging group (all fruit scents except those in the lemon group), including *Philadelphus* (orange scent), *Cytisus battandieri* (pineapple), *Freesia* (ripe plums), *Rosa wichuraiana* (green apples), *Rosa soulieana* (ripe bananas), and *Iris graminea* (apricots).

- **Animal-scented group**
  Scented of cats, dogs, foxes, goats, or human sweat, such as *Fritillaria imperialis*, *Hypericum*, oxeye daisy (*Leucanthemum vulgare*), and *Codonopsis*. Musk-scented flowers include *Rosa moschata* and *Muscari muscarimi*.

- **Honey-scented group**
  Closely related to musk-scented flowers, with a delicate, sweet fragrance, including *Buddleia*, *Sedum spectabile*, and honeysuckle (*Lonicera*).

Leaf perfume groups

Leaf scent is more subtle than that of flowers. However, while a flower's perfume reduces when dried, leaf fragrance is persistent and can increase as the water evaporates, concentrating the essential oils. Some of the same oils are found in both leaves and flowers. As a result, some leaf fragrances conform to flower-scent groupings, including many *Pelargonium*, which fall into the rose or lemon groups. Apple mint (*Mentha suaveolens*) and *Rosa rubiginosa* (formerly *R. eglanteria*) smell of apples and fall into the fruit-scented group, as does *Salvia sclarea*, a hardy biennial with leaves smelling of fresh grapefruit when bruised. Leaves also contain some different oils from flowers, such as pine scent.

- **Turpentine group**
  A resinous aroma, such as rosemary (*Rosmarinus*).

- **Camphor and eucalyptus group**
  A medicinal scent that clears the nasal passages, including sage (*Salvia officinalis*), Roman chamomile (*Chamaemelum nobile*), *Eucalyptus*, thyme (*Thymus*), and myrtle (*Myrtus*).

- **Mint group**
  A tangy, fresh scent, such as *Mentha* and *Pelargonium*.

- **Sulphur group**
  A heavy, cloying smell, including garden onions (*Allium cepa*) and garlic (*Allium sativum*).

Stems and bark

Freshly cut timber has a soft, warm fragrance, and many woody plants have fragrant stems, gum, and/or bark. Sweetgale (*Myrica gale*) has wood and leaves with a sweet, lemony fragrance when crushed. *Hebe cupressoides* has stems and leaves with a light bouquet of violets, and sweetgum (*Liquidambar styraciflua*) has a balsamic scent. Plants with scented bark fall into two categories.

- **Aromatic group**
  Includes pepper cinnamon (*Canella winteriana*), *Eucalyptus*, *Betula lenta* (a warm, spicy scent like wintergreen), and *Illicium anisatum* (incense-scented).

- **Turpentine group**
  A resinous aroma, including conifers such as fir (*Abies*), Scotch pine (*Pinus sylvestris*), and larch (*Larix*).

Roots

Several plants have fragrant roots, although the scent is not detectable unless the plants are dug up. Herb bennet (*Geum urbanum*) is an herbaceous perennial with short, thick, rhizomatous roots that smell of cloves when dried. Purple avens (*Geum rivale*) is moisture-loving with thick, rhizomatous roots smelling of chocolate. Other plants with fragrant roots include licorice (*Glycyrrhiza glabra*) and sweet flag (*Acorus calamus*), which produces a camphorlike smell and was used in the past as a strewing herb for floors. *Iris pallida* and *I.* 'Florentina' both have roots that smell strongly of violets when dried and powdered.

Fungi

Various fungi have distinctive smells, not all of them pleasant, although they tend to change as the fungus matures. Some, such as the stinkhorn (*Phallus impudicus*), attract flies to spread their spores by smelling of rotting flesh or fish. Others smell of damp forests, garlic, sulphur, goats, or musk. The more pleasant scents include cloves, anise, violet, rose, and fruit.

Seeds

Many plants have seeds that can give rich scents and flavors to food and drink, usually by crushing. Aniseed (*Pimpinella anisum*) gives a licorice flavor to cough mixtures, liqueurs, soups, candy, and cakes. Caraway seeds (*Carum carvi*) flavor bread, cakes, cheese, soups, and liqueurs. Coriander seeds (*Coriandrum sativum*) have an orangy fragrance when dry. They are used in pickles and curries and, with sugar, in the making of candy. The seeds of dill (*Anethum graveolens*) have a spicy bouquet and are added to cakes, bread, fish, and rice dishes. Fennel (*Foeniculum vulgare*) has the flavor of licorice and complements oily fish such as mackerel.

The leaves of the garlic plant (Allium sativum) *have a heavy, cloying scent and are thus classified in the sulphur group.*

How plants use scent

Everything in nature evolves for a reason, and the fragrance in plants is no exception. Scent performs two main functions: It provides protection for the plant, either from pests or desiccation, and attracts pollinating insects. But why do some plants have a strong fragrance while others have none at all? And why are there so many different fragrances? These questions can be answered by looking at the life cycle of the plants themselves and the environments they inhabit—for example, bees are attracted to the color blue, so some plants that grow in areas colonized by bees produce blue flowers and therefore have no need for scent. Natural evolution is not the only factor determining a plant's fragrance, however. Over the years, horticulturists have bred many plants to enhance or reduce certain characteristics, including scent.

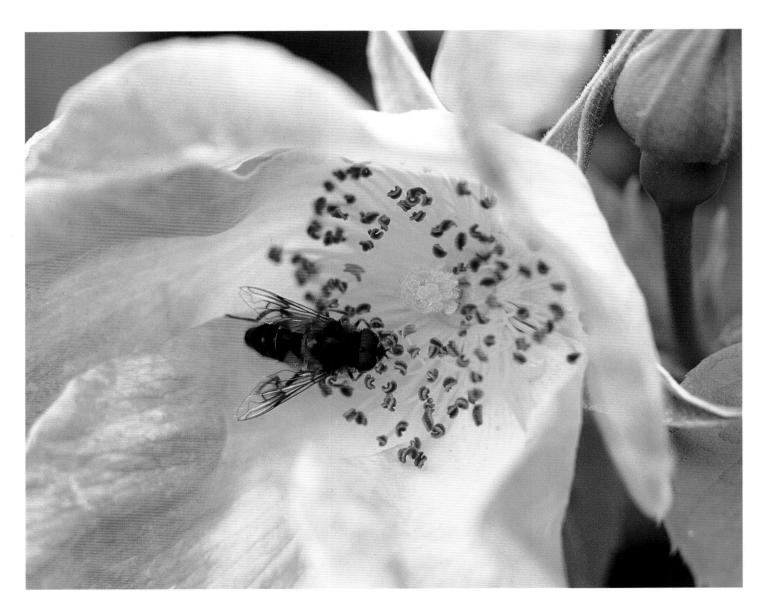

Protection

Plants can use the essential oils in their leaves and stems to deter attacks by pests and browsing animals. The oils almost become a replacement for thorns. For example, ants seem to dislike the scent of mint intensely and will avoid it at all costs, so the variety known as 'Pennyroyal' (*Mentha pulegium*) can be useful to have around the entrances to the home to deter these insects from entering.

Many highly aromatic plants originate in hot, arid areas where they protect themselves from desiccation by releasing oils that remain in a vapor immediately around the surface of the leaf. The effect is further enhanced if the leaf is covered with hairs that can trap the vapor.

Pollination

All plants rely on pollination to ensure the continuation of the species. Different plants have different methods of ensuring that pollination takes place. Some, like birch (*Betula*), oak (*Quercus*), and conifers, use wind dispersal of pollen; others, such as *Elodea*, use water. The majority, however, rely on insects. This allows cross-pollination between plants, so that genetic material is constantly mixed and the resultant plants are strong and healthy.

Scent is an important way of attracting pollinating insects. It is more noticeable on a calm, warm day, especially in a sheltered spot or under trees, since the more sheltered the location, the more the plant relies on fragrance to attract insects, because they are less likely to be brought past on the wind. Plants that grow in shaded places or that flower during the night are especially fragrant. Most night-flowering blooms open for a single night and die after fertilization. The lower temperatures and higher humidity levels of evening and nighttime trigger the release of fragrances. Many flowers that open at night, such as Italian honeysuckle (*Lonicera caprifolium*), are pale colors such as white, cream, or pale yellow, with long, tubular flower parts.

Many different insects can be involved in the pollination process, and each is attracted by a different means. Competition to attract them is fierce, and some plants have very specific relationships with the pollinating agent. A mutual dependence can evolve so that the life cycles of both insect and plant are closely connected.

Bees are attracted by certain colors and markings, so flowers such as this Rosa 'Complicata' do not need to have a strong scent to attract them.

Butterflies and moths

Both belong to the order Lepidoptera and have long, tubular mouth parts for penetrating deep into the flower. Butterflies visit flowers such as the European honeysuckle (*Lonicera periclymenum*) in the day and early evening, while moths pollinate night-flowering plants. Flowers that rely on butterflies and moths are usually strongly scented because these insects are attracted by perfume. Butterflies are especially attracted to shrubs such as lavender (*Lavandula*), privet (*Ligustrum*), lilac (*Syringa*), and *Buddleia*, and herbaceous perennials such as *Aster*.

Bees

Bees belong to the insect class Hymenoptera, have well-developed eyesight, and are primarily attracted by certain colors (particularly blue) and markings that direct the insect toward the center of the flower. Bees appear to be color blind to red and green and show little interest in flowers of these colors. Blue flowers often have very little scent, because the color is sufficient to attract the pollinating agent.

Flies

Not all insects enjoy pleasant scents. Flies of the insect class Diptera, for example, delight in disgusting smells that have no appeal to other insects. Plants that attract flies include American skunk cabbage (*Lysichiton americanus*), purple trillium (*Trillium erectum*), lords-and-ladies (*Arum maculatum*), stinking hellebore (*Helleborus foetidus*), and fetid bugbane (*Cimicifuga foetida*).

Birds

Many birds appear to be color blind to blue and green; where they are responsible for flower pollination, the predominant flower colors are crimson and gold. The color attracts the pollinators, with fragrance having no part to play.

Beetles

The few flowers that rely on pollination by beetles usually emit a fruity scent to attract them. They are also fully open because beetles have short tongues and could not otherwise reach into a tubular-shaped bloom.

Color and scent

Color and scent do not go hand-in-hand; fragrance is often a substitute for color, and the brighter the color, the less scent there is. Since both are a means of attracting pollinating insects, one element of the plant's composition is compensating for another. The heaviest fragrance occurs in white flowers and those with thick, waxy, or velvety petals. Thinner petals cannot retain essential oils, so fragrance is quickly lost. The more pigment or chlorophyll present in the petal, the less oil is produced, so those with an absence of coloration, such as lily of the valley (*Convallaria majallis*), white carnation (*Dianthus*), and pheasant's eye narcissus (*Narcissus poeticus*), contain the most oil.

The strength of fragrance in relation to flower color can be simplified, from strongest to weakest, as: white, cream, pale yellow, yellow, pale pink, mauve, and purple. Flowers that are orange, red, blue, or brown tend to have little or no fragrance because they contain so much pigment. Clematises, with a color range from white to deep purple, are a good example of the interrelationship of color and fragrance. The winter-flowering *Clematis rehderiana* (pale creamy yellow) smells like cowslips; the spring-flowering *C. armandii* (pure white) is strongly scented; and the summer-flowering *C.* 'Duchess of Edinburgh' (white) is one of the few large-flowered hybrids to have any scent. The darker forms seldom have any scent at all.

The less pigment a flower contains, the stronger its scent. White flowers such as this Clematis armandii *have the most powerful fragrances.*

Family characteristics

Plants are categorized into families by the arrangement of their floral parts, but the scent given off by members of the same family can be quite similar. For example, all the members of *Papilionaceae* (the pea family), including sweet pea (*Lathyrus odoratus*), broom (*Cytisus/Genista*), and gorse (*Ulex*), have a

lemon-vanilla fragrance. Some plant families have little or no scent, such as *Scrophulariaceae* (including *Nemesia*, *Penstemon*, *Phygelius*, and *Antirrhinum*). Scent cannot be bred naturally into these plants because the ability to produce it has not developed in their makeup. They rely entirely on brightly colored flowers to attract pollinating insects.

Hybridizing plants

The nineteenth-century Austrian botanist Gregor Mendel was the first person to analyze the characteristics passed from one generation of plants to the next. He used the pollen from one plant to fertilize another, giving a limited range of possible options in the next generation. Plants inherited features from each parent, but also characteristics from previous generations that were not obvious in either parent. He concluded that hidden characteristics, though present in each generation, could be masked by a stronger element of the same feature.

Hybridizing is the crossing of two plants to obtain a given result. In those cases where this can be virtually guaranteed to produce a similar result every time, the offspring is known as the F1 (or first-cross) generation. F1 plants have "hybrid vigor," which means they produce plants that are bigger, with larger flowers or more fragrance. F2 plants are produced by crossing two F1 hybrids, and the results are less uniform.

Breeding for scent

Pollen from a chosen variety has to be carefully applied, in isolation, to a selected mother plant, and the resultant seed must be harvested and sown. Out of a batch of seedlings, just one or two out of a thousand might be chosen because they have more fragrance. It can take several generations to achieve a desired result. Sometimes, the selection of one characteristic will outweigh others and, over a period of years, one aspect of the plant will decline. For instance, when color is bred into flowers, the scent is often lost. This happened in roses, where breeding concentrated on flower color and size and resistance to diseases such as rust. An increased desire for fragrance has led some breeders to cross-refer back through a plant's lineage to ascertain where the scent gene weakened. They can then breed back to a rose that still had a strong scent. Ideally, the fragrance can be reintroduced without losing the benefits of the modern flower.

Breeding plants for scent is a painstaking process because just one or two seedlings from a batch of thousands could have the desired fragrance.

Essential oils

Essential oils are the concentrated natural chemicals within the plant that contain fragrance. Although they are often used simply as perfume, they also have therapeutic value. When applied by massage or in baths, the oils penetrate the skin and quickly enter the bloodstream and lymphatic system. The inhalation of the aroma is also believed to affect emotions and mood. A belief in the healing powers of essential oils dates back to the earliest times. Primitive humans, for example, used antiseptic gum from trees such as conifers, balsam poplar (*Populus balsamifera*), walnut (*Juglans*), and birch (*Betula*) to ease sore throats and treat cuts. Today oils such as cinnamon, clove, verbena, geranium, lavender, and rosemary are widely used to treat a range of health problems, from headaches and colds to insomnia and anxiety.

Types of oils

Essential oils may be held within various parts of the plant, including the flower, leaf, bark, roots, and rind. Oils extracted from fragrant leaves have a greater antiseptic strength than those obtained from petals, with the exception of attar of roses, which is a strong antiseptic. The oil is stored in the leaf in several ways. It may be held deep within the leaf or in capsules that require pressure to release the oil; in cells on or near the surface, to be released when the temperature rises; or in glandular hairs on the underside of the leaf. In flowers, the oil is stored in cells from which the chlorophyll has been withdrawn, on both surfaces of the petals, although the concentration is usually greater on the upper surface. There is a wide range of alcohol and other chemicals involved in creating each individual scent derived from the essential oils of flowers.

Obtaining essential oils

Removing the essential oils from the plant without losing the fragrance is at the heart of perfume production. Commercially, this may be done by several methods, including extraction, distillation, expression, and enfleurage. If you wish to make your own essential oils rather than buy them, you can do so using a simplified home enfleurage process.

Extraction

The oil is gently washed from the flowers using a chemical solution to obtain the most concentrated essence. The solvent produces a thick, concentrated wax that is identical in perfume to that of the original flower.

Distillation

Flowers able to withstand heat and produce a large amount of scent for their weight, such as rose and orange blossom petals, are placed in a large tank, and steam is driven through them. The oil can then be separated from the water, as the two substances do not mix.

Expression

The raw material—usually citrus rind—is compressed in order to release the oil. Water is then used to separate the waste material from the oil.

The fresh flowers of Lavandula angustifolia *are used to make lavender essential oil. Lavender oil, with its sweet floral scent, is renowned for its ability to relax the body and uplift the mind.*

Enfleurage

Sometimes known as absorption, this expensive method is suitable for delicate flowers that will not withstand chemical or heat treatments, such as lily of the valley (*Convallaria majalis*), violet (*Viola*), and jasmine (*Jasminum*). These flowers continue to give off oils after harvesting, so they are laid on glass sheets and covered with vegetable oil that gradually absorbs the fragrance. The flowers are changed daily for up to a month so that the vegetable oil contains as much fragrance as possible. Alternatively, the flowers may be spread onto muslin sheets soaked in olive oil. After a month, the cloth is squeezed to remove the olive oil saturated with scent. The vegetable oil or olive oil is then treated to separate the scent.

Home enfleurage

To produce small quantities of your own essential oil, gather the dry flowers of the plant you wish to use, remove the stalks, and place the flowers in a glass jar half-filled with good-quality olive oil. After twenty-four hours, remove the flowers, squeeze them (allowing the liquid to run back into the jar), and then discard the flowers. Add some fresh flowers to the jar. Repeat this process until the oil is saturated with perfume. Finally, add an equal quantity of pure (ethyl) alcohol, screw a tight lid onto the jar, and shake daily for two weeks. The fragrant alcohol can then be poured off the olive oil and used.

Buying and storing oils

Although it can be satisfying to produce your own oil, buying essential oils is the quickest and easiest option because there are many different oils available from a wide range of producers. Always read the label before you buy to see where the company sources its ingredients and if it runs checks for purity. If the oil is labeled as "aromatherapy oil," it will probably have been mixed with a carrier oil such as grapeseed oil. Although this is necessary if you wish to apply essential oil to the skin through massage, for example, it does reduce the oil's life from years to months.

All essential oils oxidize over time, so look for oils sold in dark-tinted glass bottles and avoid any that have been on display in a hot window, because heat and sunlight accelerate the deterioration process. Try to keep the bottles sealed as much as possible and store them in a cool place such as a refrigerator. When blending your own oils, use a glass eyedropper (available from your local pharmacy) to measure the quantities of oil and always shake the bottle well before use. Remember to label the bottle, too, and include the date of purchase.

Using essential oils at home

There are many ways in which essential oils can be used around the home to have a beneficial influence on both you and your surroundings. Depending on which fragrance is selected, the effect can be relaxing or stimulating, and the effect can even be enhanced if oils are used in combination.

Baths

After a busy day in the garden, add five to ten drops of your favorite essential oil to a filled bath and then lie back and enjoy. The water should not be too hot or the fragrance will be lost quickly. An aromatherapy bath is also ideal for relieving stress, especially with a relaxing oil such as lavender. Other oils you might like to try include bergamot and jasmine for depression, neroli and ylang ylang for anxiety, eucalyptus and peppermint for headaches, and chamomile and juniper for aches and pains.

Massage

Essential oils are highly concentrated and should be diluted in a carrier oil, such as grapeseed or jojoba, for skin application. This also helps the hands to glide smoothly. The scent of the carrier oil should not overpower the essential oil—olive oil, for example, aids itchy skin but tends to be strongly scented. For every 2 oz. of carrier oil, add twenty drops of essential oil for use on the body; ten drops for use on the face; and five to ten drops for use on children. Each essential oil has its own properties and can be matched to the occasion. Try clary sage and basil for fatigue, peppermint and ginger for nausea and digestive problems, sweet marjoram and rose for insomnia, and patchouli and sandalwood to increase sex drive.

Vaporization

Ceramic burners usually consist of a shallow saucer over a tealight candle. The heat from the candle causes drops of oil (either used alone or in a small quantity of water) to evaporate and scent the air. Alternatively, place a few drops of oil in a dish of water on a radiator or in a sunny window. Eucalyptus has a refreshing scent, bergamot is stimulating, basil increases concentration, rose improves the mood, and lavender is relaxing. In the car, place a few drops of an oil such as peppermint on a small sponge or tissue to help you stay alert during a trip.

Potpourri

Refresh the scent of fading potpourri by adding a few drops of your favorite essential oil. Rose, citrus, and spice oils are ideal for this, either alone or in combination.

Perfume

Essential oils need to be mixed with alcohol in a ratio of about 1:5 oil to alcohol in order to preserve their scent as perfume. Alternatively, a few drops of oil on a tissue tucked discreetly into your clothing will last for several hours. By mixing oils together, you can create a unique fragrance to suit your own personality and preferences. Using oils in this way can also be therapeutic. If you are having trouble sleeping, for example, a few drops of lavender, basil, chamomile, or clary sage oil on your pillow or on a tissue nearby should help you relax and enjoy a good night's sleep.

Steam inhalation

Many essential oils have active antibacterial and antiseptic properties and can be used as a steam inhalant. For a cold, try adding five to eight drops of eucalyptus oil to a large bowl of hot water. Lean over the bowl, place a towel over your head, and breathe in the vapor for about ten minutes. Repeat two or three times a day.
Warning: Anyone suffering from asthma should not use steam inhalation.

Compresses

Therapeutic oils such as chamomile, lavender, rosemary, juniper, birch, and ginger can also be applied to the body using hot and cold compresses. Use hot compresses to relieve muscular aches and pains, and use cold compresses to soothe headaches and tension. Add five to ten drops of oil to the hot or cold water and stir well. Soak a cloth or towel in the water, then squeeze out the excess and place the cloth on the affected area. Leave in place until the compress begins to cool down or heat up, then repeat for up to an hour.

Warning

Do not apply undiluted essential oils to the skin, and avoid citrus oils prior to exposure to the sun. If you have sensitive skin, test first with a small amount of oil to check for a reaction. Never massage areas of the body with broken skin, rashes, swollen joints, or varicose veins. Anyone with a heart condition should avoid massage. Expectant mothers and people with high blood pressure or epilepsy should consult a qualified aromatherapist before using essential oils.

The flowering tops of Rosmarinus officinalis *produce essential oil with a pine fragrance. The antiseptic qualities of rosemary oil make it effective against skin irritations and a useful ingredient in hair tonics.*

Harvesting & drying

The flowers, leaves, seeds, roots, and bark of plants can be harvested, dried, and stored for future use. It is important to harvest different parts of the plant at different times of the year and to dry them correctly. This will ensure that the harvested plants are in the best condition, retaining as much of their fragrance, flavor, and other properties as possible. Once you have mastered this process, there are numerous books available containing recipes and remedies that use plant materials as ingredients. One of the easiest and most popular ways in which to use plant material is potpourri. This is usually a fragrant mixture of garden by-products in an ornamental bowl, and it may be dry or moist (a combination of pickled flowers and leaves).

Leaves

For the best results, it is important to harvest leaves when they are at their peak. This means that they should be mature but not beginning to show signs of aging. To make sure you get the best flavor or fragrance—from plants such as lemon verbena (*Aloysia triphylla*), *Pelargonium*, bee balm (*Monarda didyma*), rosemary (*Rosmarinus officinalis*), and sage (*Salvia officinalis*), for example—aim to harvest in midsummer before the plant flowers, although the exact timing will be dictated by the weather conditions. After flowering starts, the chemical balance within the plant changes and the oils in the leaves are not as potent. Pick leaves in the morning, after the dew has dried and the plant has begun to warm up, but before the day becomes too hot, discarding any damaged leaves and those close to flowers.

With most plants, it is easier to cut whole stems because they can be handled without damaging the individual leaves. Bundle them together in bunches of five to ten stems, depending on their thickness, and secure them with a rubber band (as the stems dry out and shrink, they often fall through the loop if they are tied with string). Hang the bunches upside down in a dark, warm, well-ventilated place, such as an airing cupboard, until they are dry. Drying time will depend on the thickness of the stems involved and can vary from days to weeks. For cooking, herb leaves should be crumbled between finger and thumb and stored in dark, airtight glass jars with labels until they are needed. For potpourri, the leaves can be left whole.

Flowers

Like leaves, flowers should also be harvested when they are at their peak. It is best to do this in the middle of a dry day, when the flowers are fully open but not beginning to fade. Remove the whole flower with some of the stalk to avoid damaging the petals, then check the petals carefully and discard any damaged ones. Place the flowers in an open container so that they do not begin to sweat, which can lead to rotting.

Dry large flowers by hanging them in bunches in a dark, warm, well-ventilated area in the same way as leaves. Lay small flowers that are difficult to hang, such as common borage (*Borago officinalis*) or violets (*Viola*), on sheets of muslin stretched over

Always harvest flowers when they are at the peak of their condition and before they begin to fade. Remove them by the stalk to avoid causing any damage to the delicate petals.

a wooden frame or metal cooling rack. Dried correctly, flowers should retain almost all of their color. Once dry, the petals or whole flowers are ready to use—in potpourri, for instance. If storing them for future use, flowers such as English lavender (*Lavandula angustifolia*) and Roman chamomile (*Chamaemelum nobile*) can be stored intact; others, like pot marigold (*Calendula officinalis*), need to have their petals removed.

Seeds

Seeds such as juniper berries, vanilla pods, dill seeds, nutmeg, and cloves should be fully ripe before harvesting, with no visible signs of green remaining. Collect them on a warm, dry day by shaking the seed head into a paper bag or cutting whole seed heads and laying them on paper in a seed tray. Put them in a dark, warm, well-ventilated location and allow them to dry. Many seeds will turn brown or black when they dry, but not all, so test them for firmness to check whether they are dry or not, rather than relying on their color. Store dried seeds in packets or envelopes in a dark, airtight jar until they are needed.

Bark

The bark of some trees, such as *Eucalyptus*, cedar (*Cedrus*), and sandalwood (*Santalum album*), peels readily and can be collected, preferably from younger stems. Do not pull at the bark or you may damage the tree, and never remove a circle of bark right around the trunk or the tree will die. Dry pieces of bark by laying them on a muslin-covered frame in a warm, dark location in the same way as flowers.

Roots

Both roots and rhizomes from plants such as Norwegian angelica (*Angelica archangelica*), ginger (*Zingiber officinale*), orris (*Iris germanica florentina*), sweet violet (*Viola odorata*), and garden valerian (*Valeriana officinalis*) should be harvested in the fall, when the foliage is dying down and the concentration of oils is at its strongest. Remove the required amount and replant the rest of the plant so that it will survive for the next season. Wash the soil from the roots, handling them very carefully to avoid damaging or bruising them. Lay the roots on baking trays and dry them in an oven, turning them regularly until they break easily, then cool and store in an airtight glass or metal container.

Drying temperature

As soon as a flower or leaf is detached from the plant, changes begin to take place within the cells because their supply of moisture is cut off. The quicker the piece of plant material can be dried, the quicker this process is stopped, trapping the oils within the cells. However, the process must be controlled, because drying too quickly, in an oven for example, allows the remaining moisture to evaporate too quickly, taking the oils with it. If dried too slowly, however, the oils are destroyed by decomposition. Ideally, flowers, leaves, seeds, and bark should be dried in a dark, warm, well-ventilated location, like an airing cupboard or warm loft, aiming for a temperature of around 80°F. The exception is roots, which can be dried in the oven at about 120°F, because they need higher temperatures in order to dry properly.

Dry potpourri

Dry potpourri mixtures are easiest to make using dried leaves, flowers, berries, spices, peel, or bark, along with a fixative to preserve the blend. Fixatives are available as powders and often have their own fragrance that must be taken into account when choosing the mixture of ingredients. The most common fixative is orrisroot, with its violet scent, and is used in a ratio of about 1 tbsp. of orrisroot to every 1 cup of plant material. Essential oils are ideal for refreshing old potpourri, but add only a few drops at a time or the fragrance will be overpowering.

The choice of plant material suitable for making potpourri is wide-ranging, so it is always possible to create a fragrance to suit your personal tastes. You can also tailor scents to different areas of the home—for example, you could opt for a warm, spicy mixture in a hallway or a sweet, floral bouquet in a bedroom. You could also design your potpourri to reflect the changing seasons (see seasonal plant directories for ideas). Listed here are just a few of the plants you might like to choose.

- **Scented flowers**
  Honeysuckle (*Lonicera*), hyacinth (*Hyacinthus*), jasmine (*Jasminum*), lavender (*Lavandula*), lilac (*Syringa*), mock orange (*Philadelphus*), rose (*Rosa*), and violet (*Viola*).

- **Aromatic leaves**
  Sweet basil (*Ocimum basilicum*), laurel (*Laurus nobilis*), bee balm (*Monarda didyma*), lemon balm (*Melissa officinalis*), mint (*Mentha*), rosemary (*Rosmarinus*), sage (*Salvia*), anise (*Myrrhis odorata*), and thyme (*Thymus*).

- **Fragrant spices, peels, and roots**
  Allspice, cinnamon, clove, ginger, nutmeg, and star anise; all types of citrus peel; roots of cowslip/primrose (*Primula veris*), sweet flag (*Acorus calamus*), and valerian (*Valeriana*).

Herb and lavender dry potpourri

1 cup English lavender flowers (Lavandula angustifolia)
½ cup dried spearmint (Mentha spicata)
½ cup sweet marjoram (Origanum majorana)
½ cup oregano flowers (Origanum vulgare)
2 tbsp. powdered orrisroot
2 tsp. lavender essential oil

Mix the ingredients together well, then place in a plastic bag for two weeks to mature, shaking regularly. Display in an ornamental bowl.

Moist potpourri

This traditional method uses the highly fragrant petals of the damask rose (*Rosa damascena*) or cabbage rose (*Rosa centifolia*) as the main ingredient and produces a potpourri that will last for several years. Partially dry the rose petals until they are leathery and halved in bulk (about two days in good weather), then layer them with sea salt in a ratio of 1 cup of salt to 3 cups of petals. Alternate layers in a bowl until it is two-thirds full, then stand it in a dark, dry, well-ventilated place for ten days until the ingredients are caked together. Break the "cake" into pieces and mix with the other ingredients in the recipe below in an airtight container. Let the mixture ferment for six weeks, stirring daily. Add any dried flowers and essential oils for the final two weeks.

Rose and spice moist potpourri

4 cups fermented rose petals (see above)
6 tbsp. powdered orrisroot
2 tbsp. ground mace
2 tbsp. ground allspice
1 tbsp. ground cloves
1 nutmeg, grated
1 cinnamon stick, loosely crushed
1 tbsp. crushed bay leaves (Laurus nobilis)
1 tbsp. citrus peel
1 cup dried rosebuds

Following the instructions outlined above, ferment all the ingredients together, except the dried rosebuds, for four weeks, then add the rosebuds and ferment for another two weeks. Transfer the potpourri to a decorative container. Cover the container when not in use to preserve the potpourri's fragrance.

Roses (Rosa) *are a traditional ingredient in potpourri. The dried petals can be used in dry potpourri or they can be fermented and used as the basis of a moist potpourri that will last several years.*

DESIGNING A FRAGRANT GARDEN DESIGNING A FRAGRANT GARDEN DESIGNING A FRAGRANT GARDEN DESIGNING A FRAGRANT GARDEN DESIGNING A FRAGRANT GARDEN...

chapter two

2

Assessing your garden

Whether you are giving an old garden a new look or starting from scratch with bare ground, you will need to ascertain a few basic points to help you choose the right plants for the right locations. Remember that a garden is a long-term investment in both time and money, so it makes sense to do a little research before you begin. It will pay dividends over the years, with your plants thriving rather than struggling or, worse, having to be replaced. You also need to assess the garden in terms of existing features and factors such as privacy and size, and adjust your design accordingly—a well-placed hedge can increase the privacy of your garden and reduce the amount of noise entering it, as well as introduce fragrance.

Orientation and location

The orientation of a garden is the direction it faces—that is, the direction from which it receives the most direct sunlight. You can use a compass to be exact, or simply watch the progress of the sun throughout the day, noting which areas are the hottest and which get no sun at all. You have no choice over the orientation, but it will influence the plants you can use in these areas, since shade-lovers will scorch in the sun and sun-lovers will become drawn and sickly in the shade.

Another factor to take into account is the location of your garden. Do you live in an urban area where temperatures are usually warmer and the situation more sheltered, an exposed rural setting where the temperature is cooler and frost more common, or a coastal area affected by salt-laden winds but less-severe temperatures? All of these factors will affect which plants will do well in your particular garden.

Soil type

Knowing what type of soil you have will also help you determine the plants that best suit your garden. To identify the type of soil, rub some between your fingers. If it does not stick together, you probably have sandy or silty soil; if it feels gritty but does stick together, it is most likely to be a loam soil; if it sticks together readily with a shiny surface, it is clay soil. Loam soils are ideal for most plants. Sandy and silty soils drain freely and are therefore suitable for plants that can cope with dry conditions. Clay soils drain slowly and are perfect for moisture-loving plants.

pH level

As soil forms, it is influenced by local factors such as the underlying rock type—these have an effect on the soil's acidity or alkalinity. The exact nature of your soil can be measured on what is known as the pH scale—a scale from 1 to 14, with 1 being the most acidic and 14 the most alkaline—using a small soil-testing kit available from garden centers. Every plant has a pH range in which it will thrive, and another in which it can survive. A pH of 6.5 to 7 is regarded as neutral, or suitable for a wide range of plants. Below this, the soil will be too acidic for lime-loving plants (calcicoles) such as *Dianthus*. Above pH 7, the soil will be too alkaline for acid-loving plants (calcifuges)

If you know the pH level of your soil, you can choose plants that will thrive in those conditions. This Rhododendron cubittii *prefers acidic soil with a pH level of less than 6.5.*

such as *Rhododendron*. If your soil has extreme pH levels, the only way to grow plants from the opposite group is to keep them in containers, where you have complete control over the growing conditions. Knowing the pH level of your soil can save you from making costly mistakes, like buying a plant that is unsuitable for the conditions and is unlikely to survive.

To test your soil, take five small samples (free from stones and plant debris) from a depth of about 4 in. at different points around the garden. Mix the samples together in a plastic bag. Following the manufacturer's instructions provided with the soil-testing kit, test a small amount of soil from the bag. Once the test is complete, the color of the clear liquid in the sample can be compared against the chart supplied with the kit to show the overall pH level of your garden. Alternatively, a single test sample will show the pH level of a specific part of the garden.

Existing features

Unless you are designing a new garden for a bare patch of ground, you will probably have to work around existing features. Some of these, such as a greenhouse on a brick base, will be fixed, but others might be movable, even if they have to remain on site. Wooden sheds, for example, may be moved to another location, provided a stable new base can be created. When drawing a plan of the garden (see page 44), remember to indicate features such as these right away so that you do not overlook them later when you are creating your design. There are some existing features, such as air conditioners, compost containers, and trash cans, that are best hidden from view, and planning a new design is the ideal time to hide or disguise them. Tall plants, climbers, trellises, or woven screens are all methods of making what could be an unsightly area into an attractive one.

Privacy

Many people regard the garden as an extension of the living area—a room outdoors. As such, the need for privacy while entertaining or relaxing is more important than ever. At the same time, new houses and gardens are getting smaller and more closely packed, making privacy in the garden increasingly difficult to attain. Careful planning is therefore vital if you are going to create a garden that is both pleasing to the eye and comfortable to use.

It is natural to want to position your seating area in a sunny spot, so before you begin your design, sit there and assess how exposed it will be and how much that matters to you.

Consider the possible solutions and try to visualize them in place. For example, a neighboring bedroom window can be screened with an upright plant, perhaps a small tree or upright conifer. More general exposure might warrant a hedge that can be allowed to grow just high enough to screen you without causing disputes with your neighbors over loss of light. Alternatively, you could place a screen immediately around the seating area itself, giving privacy while you are there but keeping the rest of the garden open. If these features are incorporated at the planning stage, there will be no need for a potentially expensive redesign later on when you realize there is a problem.

Boundaries

Most gardens have some form of boundary to mark the extent of the property, and larger gardens may have inner boundaries to divide the garden into discrete sections. The type of boundary used—such as walls, fences, or hedges—can have a dramatic impact on how the garden looks and feels. In terms of fragrance, a hedge around the perimeter of the garden or around an area within it is ideal. Hedges are less costly than walls, although not as long-lasting. The big bonus of using a hedge, however, is that many fragrant plants can be grown as hedges, either as a single variety (see pages 144–45) or mixed as a tapestry hedge.

Tapestry hedges mean that you can combine plants that have different seasons of interest, although their growth rates need to be fairly well matched or one may swamp another. Once the plants are established, you can extend the interest still further by growing climbers through the hedge to flower when the rest of the hedge is not in season. Choose small- or medium-sized varieties that will not overwhelm the hedge, and avoid twiners such as honeysuckle (*Lonicera*), which can strangle other plants.

Prickly fragrant plants such as *Rosa rugosa* and *Mahonia aquifolium* are ideal for growing as a low boundary hedge to deter unwanted visitors or to prevent people from cutting across the garden. Both have attractive, very fragrant blooms followed by colorful fruit later in the year, giving two seasons of interest. *Mahonia* is also evergreen.

Even if you have existing walls or fences that you wish to keep, you can choose to grow a hedge alongside them in order to introduce fragrance. A simpler solution is to grow aromatic climbers along the boundary, using a decorative trellis to train the plants if necessary. If the boundary in question is an open fence, this will also provide some additional privacy.

Paths

Spend some time moving around the garden and working out the routes you are most likely to use. Mark on your plan of the garden any existing paths that you wish to keep, and bear them in mind when drawing up your planting scheme so that the paths become fragrant journeys through your garden. You can also create additional paths and even change the existing ones altogether if they are not suitable to your needs and tastes. If you do not like an existing path but do not want to go to the expense and effort of changing it, you will need to think of ways to incorporate it into your garden design so that it becomes an unobtrusive and even desirable feature. For example, installing an archway covered with overhanging aromatic plants can draw the eye upward and minimize an unattractive path below.

Small gardens

Many houses have only small gardens, particularly newly built ones. However, there are several tricks you can employ in your garden design to make a small area seem larger than it is. For example, you can use increasingly shorter plants as you go farther away from the house. This deceives the viewer into thinking that all the plants in the garden are the same height and that those at the end of the garden are farther away than they really are. Similarly, you can use large-flowered varieties nearby and small-flowered ones at a distance. Another good trick is to keep bright colors close by and use paler ones farther away, so that they appear to blur into the distance and make the end of the garden indistinct.

You can also use shaped trellises on walls to give an increased sense of perspective. Start near the house with a trellis that covers the wall from top to bottom, then decrease its size as you move farther away. The mind expects the trellis to be the same size along its length, so the smaller trellis in the distance looks as if it is even farther away than it actually is. Another simple illusion is to use mirrors. These can be partly hidden behind plantings to give the impression that the viewer is catching a glimpse of another part of the garden through a small window. Align the mirror so that the viewer does not immediately see his or her own reflection, or the effect will be spoiled.

A large, solid hedge divides this garden into areas with distinctly different characters. The foreground is filled with a lively profusion of flowers, while the stone pagoda hints at a more tranquil area in the distance.

Choosing a style

Although you need to keep in mind the factors discussed in Assessing Your Garden (see pages 34–37), the style of plants you choose will, to a large extent, be a matter of personal taste. You should start by deciding what you want from your plants. Are you aiming for fragrance throughout the garden, or would you prefer to incorporate scented plants among unscented ones? Do you want all the fragrance to come from flowers, or are you including aromatic foliage? Do you want color, interest, and fragrance throughout the year or only in certain seasons? Also take into account whether you want to use any of the plants outside of the garden. For example, do you want herbs for cooking or cut flowers to display within the home? Time spent on this part of the planning process will reap rich rewards in the years to come.

Timing fragrance

Depending on when and how much you are likely to use your garden, it may not be necessary to plan for fragrance throughout the year. If, for instance, you rarely venture outside during the winter, then you can devote more attention to plants that are at their best during the other seasons. Alternatively, if fragrance is particularly important to you at a certain time of year, you can concentrate specifically on that season. People who suffer during the dark days of winter, for example, may find it beneficial to pick sprigs of fragrant plants to bring indoors at this time. When we think of fragrance, we usually think of flowers. But plants with fragrant fruits are also a good way of extending seasonal fragrance and interest in the garden when the main flowering season may have ended. Use the plant directories at the end of the seasonal chapters to help you plan scent according to your needs. It is also worth thinking about the time of day that you use your garden. Growing some night-scented plants, particularly near the house, walkways, or patios, is a good way of enjoying the fragrance of your garden during the evening.

- **Plants with fragrant fruits**

  Drimys winteri, Gaultheria shallon, Helianthus annuus, Illicium majus, Laurus nobilis, Monodora myristica, Podocarpus andinus, Sassafras officinale, Syzygium aromaticum, Zanthoxylum americanum.

- **Night-scented fragrant plants**

  Gladiolus tristis, Hesperis fragrans, Lonicera caprifolium, Mirabilis jalapa, Oenothera triloba, Petunia integrifolia, Silene noctiflora, Sisyrinchium odoratissimum, Verbena teucrioides, Zaluzianskya villosa.

Herb gardens

The use of herbs, both in cooking and in medicine, dates back to the earliest civilizations, and herbs are now undergoing a revival, with an ever-increasing range available. Many herbs originate in the Mediterranean region and therefore grow best in an open, sunny site with well-draining soil. Most herbs need very little space, so you can grow a wide variety in a small area of the garden or you can grow them in containers. Traditional herb gardens are designed so that they can be accessed easily throughout the year, with paths of brick or gravel to allow the

Lonicera and rosemary, intermingled with unscented plants, are used to bring fragrance to a rustic seat in a cottage-style garden.

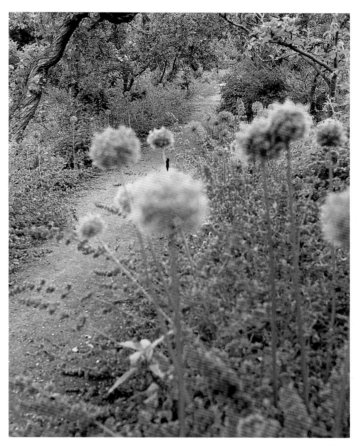

Allium and Nepeta provide colorful and fragrant ground cover along this path, enticing visitors to explore farther into the garden.

plants to be picked. These may be laid in a pattern based on circles, squares, diamonds, or diagonals. Many herb gardens are therefore planted according to a formal structure like a traditional knot garden. However, if you would prefer a less structured look, you could plant the herbs more randomly and use a mixture of paths and stepping-stones to access them.

- **Herbs suitable for growing in containers**

  Allium schoenoprasum, Crocus sativus, Laurus nobilis, Mentha x piperata f. citrata, Mentha spicata var. crispa, Monarda didyma, Myrtus communis, Ocimum basilicum, Tanacetum parthenium, Thymus x citriodorus.

- **Herbs suitable for making a lawn**

  Chamaemelum nobile, Chamaemelum nobile 'Treneague,' Mentha arvensis, Mentha pulegium, Mentha requienii, Thymus praecox, Thymus pseudolanuginosus, Vinca minor.

Cutting gardens

The keen flower arranger needs a ready supply of fresh flowers and foliage to cut throughout the year so that the house is constantly supplied with natural fragrance. Annual and perennial plants are ideal for this, but some shrubs are more tolerant than others of this kind of attention. Access to all the plants is important, and stepping-stones within the beds are an easy solution. An important thing to note is that this is a labor-intensive style of gardening; plants that are constantly being required to replace cut growth need regular and intensive feeding or their reserves will become depleted and the plant may die.

Annual gardens

Many fragrant annual plants can be dried for use in potpourri and dried flower arrangements. Since annual plants grow, flower, and die within a single season, it is possible to condition the soil regularly when the bed is empty. There should be little problem with seedlings from a previous batch of plants appearing the following year, because the flowers and seed heads should be harvested for drying before the seed is shed (see pages 28–31).

Mixed plants

By far the most popular type of garden is one that encompasses a wide range of plants: deciduous and evergreen; flowering and foliage; woody (trees and shrubs) and nonwoody (bulbs, annuals, and perennials). By having such a wide range, there can be something of interest throughout the year. In general, a garden such as this is designed with smaller plants at the front of borders and beds, and larger ones at the rear. However, it is important to remember that in winter it is not always easy to step onto the soil, and in order to appreciate the fragrance of a plant at this time, it may need to be situated near a path or door. Make full use of winter-flowering shrubs that are not interesting during the summer by planting a small- or medium-sized climber to scramble through them. The climber will be dormant in winter when the shrub flowers but will come into bloom itself during the summer months. It is possible to combine the beauty of both fragrance and water in the garden. Scented plants can be used to surround a water feature such as a fountain, pond, or pool—this is particularly effective if the feature is sited near seating. Alternatively, fragrant water-dwelling plants can be grown in the water to become an intrinsic part of the feature.

Use fragrant plants to bring scent to mixed borders. Here, roses provide a backdrop to a summer border that includes Allium, Salvia, *and* Paeonia.

Basic design principles

Beautiful gardens can look as if they were made by the hand of nature alone, with plants growing alongside each other in perfect balance and harmony. This is sometimes the case, but more often such gardens are the result of careful design. Although anyone can produce a garden design, not all designs are destined to be successful when the garden is actually created. Whether you opt for a formal, geometric design or a more rambling, natural look, there are certain basic principles that should be observed if you are to achieve a garden that fulfills all your needs. Questions of balance, harmony, rhythm, and scale all need to be addressed. Similarly, it is important to think of the garden as a three-dimensional space, taking into account the height of each feature and plant, as well as the length, width, and density.

Balance

Each element within the garden occupies space, both physically and visually. Balance is the art of making sure that one area of the garden does not outweigh another. Aim to have each busy area of plants balanced by a corresponding area of calm, open ground. This may be a lawn or some gravel, paving, or decking. Each area of bright color needs a complementary area of muted color, both to make it stand out and to rest the eye when you look away. Without this, the garden could feel crowded, overwhelming, and even claustrophobic. There will be no opportunity to stand back and admire the beauty of the plants, and their effect may be lost.

Harmony and rhythm

In music, harmony and rhythm give life to the work, a sense that all the elements flow together as part of the whole, and there is no discord. In the garden, harmony and rhythm serve the same purpose, but visually. To achieve a harmonious garden, it is best to follow a common theme throughout the design, rather than add in lots of disparate elements. For example, if you start off with curves, keep curves; do not use straight lines. Likewise, if you start with a rigid geometric pattern, do not be tempted to introduce a curve. It is easier to create a successful, flowing design with blocks of planting rather than individual plants, because there is more visual space between the centers of color. You can then use individual plants as specimens to highlight and accentuate the surrounding block.

A lawn serves the same purpose in the garden that carpeting does indoors—it flows through the different elements of the garden and links them together, just as carpet flows from one room to another to unify an interior decoration scheme. Paving performs the same function. Always try to make your linking feature—whether it is lawn or paving—flow through the design. If you dot it here and there, you will break up the rhythm of the scheme and the whole effect will become disjointed.

Scale

Keeping each feature within the garden in scale with the others, and with the size of the garden itself, will ensure that no single element becomes too dominant. A large tree or pergola will be out of scale in a small garden and will take up so much space

This rose garden uses a circular design to create a rhythmic flow around the beds of flowers and has a statue in the center to create a focal point. The arches are positioned symmetrically to keep the design balanced.

that something else will have to be sacrificed. In a large garden, a tiny pergola will be swamped by the features surrounding it, and its effect will be ruined. In a small garden, you can use smaller varieties of plants to scale everything down and give the impression of more room. In a long, thin garden, it is a good idea to use smaller plants farther away to make the garden seem even longer; conversely, putting taller plants at the far end of the garden will make it appear visually closer.

The third dimension

When designing your garden, it is important not to think in just two dimensions; use the third dimension, height, as well. Height can be found in many places. Walls, fences, and trellises can be used around the edge of the garden or introduced in the center. Obelisks, wigwams, and pillars can be inserted in borders, and hanging containers can be attached to posts and filled with trailing plants that will reach down to the plant layer below.

You can use taller plants, or structures with plants covering them, to divide the garden into sections so that the whole garden is not visible at once—the viewer will be tempted to walk into it to see what is around the corner. You may not have the space to divide the garden into entirely separate rooms, but, even in relatively small gardens, you can create compartments.

Focal points

A statue, water feature, or special plant can be used as a means of drawing the eye of the observer into the garden and to a desired area. This is useful if there is another, more unsightly feature that you wish to deflect attention away from. If the garden is small, select a scaled-down statue or feature to maintain the element of perspective. Blocks of plants, rather than single plants, can have the same effect, especially if the flowers or foliage are brightly colored.

Planting opportunities

The biggest problem that many gardeners face today is a lack of space—there is always one more plant to be squeezed in somewhere. This is where your imagination can come to the forefront. If there is an area of paving, leave gaps between the bricks or stones and plant low-growing subjects into them that can tolerate being stepped on occasionally. Thyme (*Thymus*) is an excellent plant for such situations because it releases a delicious scent when it is bruised, and is remarkably resilient. Planting pockets in walls can be filled with trailing thymes, which will thrive in the good drainage.

Wherever you have an established shrub or climber that is dull during part of the year, look for a plant you can grow up through it to flower during the required season. For instance, *Pyracantha* flowers in spring and has brightly colored berries in winter, but it is not particularly interesting at other times of the year. By planting a summer- or autumn-flowering *Clematis* to grow through its branches, you can have colorful flowers in summer, and the *Pyracantha* will support the *Clematis* as it grows. When pairing two plants in this way, you need to make sure that they are well matched, or the climber may swamp the host. Honeysuckle (*Lonicera*), for instance, is a strong-growing climber that will strangle all but the most vigorous hosts. The smaller-growing varieties of climbers are ideal.

Basic plan drawing

Once you have assessed your garden, chosen your garden style, and considered the basic principles of garden design (see previous sections of this chapter and above), you need to draw a plan of your garden. There is no need to view this as a difficult task, because with a piece of paper, pencil, and something to measure with, it is actually very easy. Doing it, however, will give you the opportunity to see how your ideas look when they are marked out and will provide a point of reference afterward if you lose any plant labels.

Working from fixed points, such as the corners of the house, measure the distance to various points around the garden. Use at least two measurements for each element of the garden, taken from different places, so that you can pinpoint these elements exactly when you transfer them onto paper. You can use a long tape measure for this or simply walk it out—but make sure only one person does the walking, because no two peoples' strides will be the same length. It is easiest to draw the plan on squared paper, using an appropriate scale—one square on the paper equal to 3 ft. or one stride, for example.

Once you are sure that you have been reasonably accurate, mark the edges of the house and garden in pencil on a large piece of paper. Add any existing features of the garden that are not going to be moved (a greenhouse on a brick base, for example). It is also a good idea to draw a pointer on the plan to show where north is, because this will help jog your memory about sunny borders when you come to finalize your choice of plants. Once you are satisfied with your drawn plan of the existing garden, go over the lines in ink. You are now ready to begin designing your new garden.

Sketch out your ideas on the plan in pencil. You may wish to photocopy the ink drawing of the plan several times in case you need to start again or wish to compare several design plans (always save an unmarked master copy for this reason). When you are satisfied, move outside and begin laying out the design on the ground with whatever materials you have available. For example, you could use a garden hose for paths, canes for fencing, strings and pegs for borders and beds, and balloons or boxes for shrubs. Doing this will help you see how your design might look in situ—your neighbors may think you have gone a little crazy, but this is the time to find out whether what you have in mind will work.

Stand back, assess the garden carefully, and make any necessary adjustments. For example, you may find that you have over- or underestimated the size of a feature. It is much easier to decide now than halfway through construction, especially if you are ordering materials such as concrete, paving slabs, or topsoil, all of which are difficult to deal with if you order too much.

Detailed planting schemes

When you have finished the basic design plan, you need to draw up detailed planting schemes for each area of the garden. So, for example, if you have indicated on the basic plan that you are going to have a flower bed near the house, you then need to plan exactly which flowers you are going to use and where they will be sited in relation to each other. This will help you ensure that the chosen plants have sufficient room to grow, that taller plants will not hide smaller ones from view, and so on. (See pages 46–49 for specific ideas on fragrant plants.)

Maintenance requirements

Before you put your plan into action, spend some time assessing how much maintenance your new garden will need. The following chapters outline the various jobs that may need to be carried out each season. Read them carefully and consider how much or how little maintenance your particular design will involve. Be realistic about the amount of maintenance work you are willing to do—there is no point in going ahead with a wonderful garden design simply to watch it fall into neglect in the years to come.

The plants growing alongside this path will need regular pruning to keep them in check. Always consider how much maintenance a garden design will require before beginning to plant.

Making the most of fragrance

There are many different benefits to be gained from growing aromatic plants, and because scents are open to such personal interpretation, each person may appreciate different ones. For most of us, the main benefit of entering a fragrant garden on a mild day is the feeling of rejuvenation that it engenders, an uplifting of the spirit that makes us feel happy, healthy, and content. Scents are extraordinarily evocative and can bring to mind memories of childhood or special places or people, and their power should never be underestimated. Each area of the garden should be treated individually when it comes to introducing fragrance, but the one element they all require is shelter. The more sheltered the position, the stronger the scent will be.

Near the house

In the area immediately outside the house, the places to concentrate on are around the windows and doors, especially the ones you open regularly during the summer. Fragrant climbers are ideal for training on the walls of the house, including *Wisteria*, star jasmine (*Trachelospermum*), roses (*Rosa*), and honeysuckle (*Lonicera*). The exact choice of plant, however, will be largely governed by the orientation of the house, because different plants can tolerate different conditions.

Try to select the right plant for the location. For instance, if you are looking for a plant to add fragrance to a bedroom, choose one like honeysuckle (*Lonicera*). This produces most of its scent during the evening because it is pollinated mainly by moths; therefore, it is ideal for growing near a room that is occupied mainly at night. In winter, when you may use only the main door to the house, plant a *Daphne* or *Viburnum* nearby so that you can smell it each time you go in or out. This is particularly useful if you tend not to venture into your garden a great deal during cold weather—remember, there is always a way to benefit from fragrant plants, whatever the weather. If you enjoy cooking, keep a range of your favorite herbs within easy reach of the kitchen door so that you can cut some easily and quickly.

If your living room has doors opening onto the garden, aim for a range of plants that will provide scent throughout late spring, summer, and fall, when the doors will be opened regularly. Use every option in terms of climbers, ground cover, and containers to extend the season whenever possible.

Along paths

Paths are an essential part of the garden. They take us to important destinations such as the shed, compost heap, and trash cans, and also transport us around the different areas of planting so that we can enjoy the garden to the fullest. Many paths are attractive features in themselves, but even the most dull-looking path can be enlivened with careful planting. Use an edging of fragrant, low-growing plants that can be clipped back if they start to encroach on the path itself—pansies (*Viola*), thyme (*Thymus*), chamomile (*Chamaemelum*), swan river daisies (*Brachycome*), and lavender (*Lavandula*) are all suitable.

This lemon tree (Citrus limon) *is perfectly located near French doors, so its fragrance can be enjoyed both in the home and in the garden. You can put large containers on casters so that they are easy to move.*

If you are building a path from scratch, you could leave planting gaps at intervals along its length so that low-growing plants can be inserted to break up any hard lines even further. However, this may not be advisable if the path is regularly used to carry items such as trays of food, which can obscure your sight of the path.

Around sitting areas

Patios and decks may be treated in the same way as paths, bringing the plants over the edges so that there are no hard lines on view and you get as much fragrance from the garden as possible. One of the most enchanting ways in which to enjoy fragrant plants is to turn the seating area into a scented arbor where you can sit, relax, and appreciate the splendor of your garden. An arbor spilling over with scented roses (*Rosa*) is a truly romantic setting.

Near the dining area

There are many reasons for using fragrant plants around an outdoor eating area, all of which will influence the plants used. If you often dine there during the day, when you need shade from the heat of the sun, use a leafy climber such as *Wisteria*. If you use the area in the evening, then the emphasis changes to plants that have scent at that time of day, such as honeysuckle (*Lonicera*) and night-scented stock (*Matthiola longipetala*).

If you cook outdoors on a barbecue, you might need a range of fragrant and tasty herbs nearby. In the heat of the day, these smell wonderful as they release their essential oils into the air, and they are ready to use when you cook. Some plants are useful for their insect-repellent qualities. Ants, for example, dislike the scent of mint and will avoid it if they can, so low-growing pennyroyal (*Mentha pulegium*) can be used around the edge of the seating area to deter them.

Around special features

A successful garden usually has distinct areas of interest, and one of the easiest ways to achieve this is to introduce special features and focal points at carefully selected locations. This could be a statue or a water feature, for instance. A good way to use fragrance to complement special features is to build up the aroma gradually as you near the feature, so that from a distance there is just a hint of scent and, as you draw nearer, the aroma grows until it reaches its climax at the feature itself. However, try not to go overboard, because an overpowering fragrance will make it unpleasant to linger there.

The plants you choose to position around the special features in your garden should be those with the fragrance you most enjoy. Obviously, focal points such as a water feature will have a limited number of plants to choose from, but there are still enough to suit most tastes, from the many strikingly beautiful water lilies to pretty cinnamon-scented sweet flag (*Acorus calamus*). Remember, too, that you can plant fragrant flowers in the area around the water feature, though you need to make sure that the different scents complement one another.

Scent during the evening

There is nothing nicer than making the most of a warm summer's evening by relaxing in the garden, and if the air can be perfumed as well, so much the better. There are many plants that are fragrant throughout daylight hours, but some plants are scented only in the evening because they are pollinated by night-flying insects such as moths.

The pretty pink and white flowers of Lilium speciosum *release a sweet fragrance in the evening, perfect for dining and seating areas.*

Varieties of honeysuckle (*Lonicera*), *Nicotiana*, garden mignonette (*Reseda odorata*), night-scented stock (*Matthiola longipetala*), *Mirabilis jalapa*, lilies (*Lilium*), *Phlox*, evening primrose (*Oenothera*), roses (*Rosa*), and arugula (*Hesperis*) all smell delightful during the evening. Use them near open windows and doors, and near the outdoor dining areas.

Fragrant plants for containers

The great attraction of growing fragrant plants in containers is that they are movable, so you can position them wherever they will give the best effect. If you have steps leading to a door, smaller containers can be placed on each side at the base of the steps so that the scent accompanies you as you climb. More scented plants can be placed in containers at the doorway itself.

On the patio or sitting area, containers can be moved to the fore as they come into bloom and retired to the back as they fade, so you have constant interest and fragrance. They can be moved nearer to the dining area if you are entertaining, or placed next to a window if the weather is not warm enough to sit outside.

To make moving a large container easier, you can fit small casters to the base before you plant. Then it can be moved into position quickly and easily. This will allow you to use taller plants as a mobile screen—such as near the dining area—to give privacy. Climbing plants grown on a tripod, wigwam, or obelisk are effective for this, as are small trees. Almost any plant will grow in a container as long as it is well cared for. Even fruit trees such as apples (*Malus*) are suitable, as long as you select a variety grown on a dwarfing rootstock to limit the growth rate and remember to water, feed, and repot it regularly.

Planting for fragrance year-round

There are plants in flower during each month of the year, even in the depths of winter—all you have to do is seek them out. Surprisingly, the ones that flower in winter often have a stronger fragrance than those that flower in summer. This is because a shortage of pollinating insects means that the plant has to work harder to attract them. However, the winter-flowering types can often look quite dull during the rest of the year, so plant them in a position where the scent can be easily appreciated in winter (close to a path), yet with a colorful companion for interest during the rest of the year. Alternatively, you could plant a small *Clematis texensis* to grow through a winter-flowering shrub such as *Viburnum farreri*, for instance, so that it flowers in the late summer, giving an extra season of interest.

Indoor fragrance

Plants can provide fragrance indoors in several ways. Dried flowers, petals, and leaves can be used in formal arrangements and bowls of potpourri (see page 30); cut flowers look wonderful in a vase or formal arrangement; and fragrant flowering plants may be grown in the house or sunroom. Each of these looks attractive and fills the room with natural fragrance, although it is important to be aware that some sweet, cloying fragrances can become overpowering and are best used in larger, cooler areas of the house than in confined, warm ones.

Climbers have been trained up the walls of this house to bring fragrance right to the bedroom window—a perfect way to wake up.

THE FRAGRANT GARDEN IN SPRING THE FRAGRANT GARDEN IN SPRING THE FRAGRANT GARDEN IN SPRING THE FRAGRANT GARDEN IN SPRING...

chapter three

3

Plants for spring

Spring is the time of year when the garden comes to life. Within just a few weeks, it is transformed from a seemingly lifeless area into one that is bursting with color and energy. The plants vie with one another to produce the best show of flowers and new leaves, and the air is heavy with perfume and the drone of bees. A wide variety of plants provide spring fragrance; as a result, it is more difficult to know what to leave out of your planting design than what to put into it. Two of the most dramatic groups at this time are trees, due to their larger size, and bulbs, because of their beautiful shapes and colors. The choice of tree will depend on the size of your garden, while the range of spring-flowering fragrant bulbs is staggering.

Large trees

Trees provide privacy, improve the atmosphere, and take the garden into the third dimension of height. Large gardens can cope with large trees such as the common horse chestnut (*Aesculus hippocastanum*), which has small, sweetly fragrant flowers in candle-like clusters. The medium-sized garden has the widest range of choice, with trees like *Malus hupehensis, Prunus* x *yedoensis* and *Magnolia* x *soulangeana*, all of which provide a wonderful display during the early part of the new season.

Small trees

Small gardens or areas such as terraces, where the plants may be confined to containers, require a more careful choice of trees. *Laburnum* x *watereri* 'Vossii' and *Arbutus andrachne* grow into attractive small trees; both prefer to be planted in the ground. For the container, fruit trees grown on dwarf rootstocks are an ideal means of combining fragrance in spring with fruit later in the year. Apples (*Malus*) growing on a dwarf rootstock such as M27 will do well in containers. Delicately scented small varieties of peach (*Prunus persica*), apricot (*Prunus armeniaca*), and nectarine (*Prunus persica* var. *nucipersica*) are also suitable.

Bulbs for outdoor fragrance

You can color-coordinate your borders or pots, or opt for a riot of different shades. Sizes range from just 1 in. high to 20 in., so choose varieties that will be in scale with their surroundings. Keep some of the smaller ones in attractive pots and place them in full view when the flowers are at their best, then move them to a quiet corner of the garden as they fade to allow them to die down. Daffodils and other members of the *Narcissus* family are highly fragrant and have the advantage that the flowers can be picked and brought indoors.

Bulbs for indoor fragrance

One of the most popular bulbs for indoor fragrance is *Hyacinthus*, which is available in white and shades of red, blue, yellow, and orange. Hyacinths can be bought as dormant "forced" bulbs (prepared for early flowering) in autumn and grown in a cool, dark place over the winter, ready for flowering in spring, or bought in spring as pregrown plants just before flowering. You can combine several bulbs together in a large container for a dramatic and more fragrant effect.

Spring-flowering Magnolia x soulangeana *'Rustica Rubra,' with its creamy pink flowers and strong scent, is ideal for a medium-sized garden.*

Spring weather and its effects

At this time of year the weather can be deceptive, with high daytime temperatures and bright sunlight that encourage rapid plant growth, followed by plunging night temperatures and late frosts that can scorch it off again. Frosts can catch even experienced gardeners unaware, particularly in late spring when it is easy to be deceived by the warm days into believing the cold weather has passed. It is important to be aware that this can cause problems and to take precautions to avoid losing shoot tips, leaves, or even whole plants to the cold (see Windbreaks, page 55, and Using a Cloche, page 57). Sheltering plants from the wind helps to emphasize their fragrance because the essential oils are not blown away. The flowers also last longer when they are not subject to strong winds that shatter the blooms.

*The Grecian strawberry tree (*Arbutus andrachne*) is perfect for a small garden. Named for its strawberry-like fruits that appear in autumn, it also produces delicate, honey-scented white flowers in spring.*

Jobs for spring

Spring is one of the busiest times of the gardener's year. In fact, so much needs to be done that it can be hard to decide where to start. Everything seems to need attention during spring, from tiny seedlings that require regular watering and protection from cold winds to full-grown plants that need feeding and pruning in order to flower well. You should also spend time controlling the growth of weeds. They seem to grow overnight at this time of year and the battle to curb them is constant. This is the time to assess whether to apply a thick mulch to control weeds or to plant densely leaved ground-cover plants instead. You will need to prioritize the various jobs that are required, giving attention to whichever is the most urgent at any particular time.

Feeding

To ensure that there are nutrients in the soil when the roots begin to search for them, feed plants during the spring. This will provide the plants with the minerals they need to grow, flower, and fruit, as well as withstand attack by pests or disease. The top priority is to give them a feed of general fertilizer. The winter rain will have washed whatever nutrients were in the soil the previous year down beyond the reach of most roots, so the nutrients need to be replaced if the plants are to perform well. The danger of not feeding is cumulative rather than immediate, so although there is no noticeable effect if you do not feed plants during the spring, the growth will gradually slow and the flowers will be smaller.

Plants need a range of nutrients to grow well, from the main elements, nitrogen (N), phosphorus (P), and potassium (K), to minor trace elements, including magnesium and copper. On the fertilizer bag or container, the three main elements are given in a ratio to one other, because each has a different part to play in plant growth and may be needed at a different time of year. In basic terms, plants need nitrogen for shoots (healthy top growth, larger leaves), phosphorus for roots, and potassium for fruits and flowers. Most plants benefit from more nitrogen and phosphorus in spring, when they are growing quickly, but less in summer, when the emphasis changes to potassium. For the largest and most fragrant flowers, increased potassium should be applied from late spring onward. If scented foliage is more important to you, use a high nitrogen feed during late spring.

Pruning

Plants need to be pruned in order to flower well. If you are hesitant about which shrubs to prune and when to do so, aim to prune after flowering so that the plant has a full year to recover, ready for flowering again the following year. By removing the shoot that has flowered, you will encourage the plant to produce new replacement stems that will flower in years to come.

Weed control

The battle against weeds is never-ending in the garden, especially in spring when their rate of growth seems to outstrip everything else. However, there are ways of reducing the amount of time you have to spend pulling them out. Like any other seedlings, they need light to grow, so smothering the soil will help. You can

Feeding plants is important if you are to achieve a good show of healthy flowers. Concentrate on providing nitrogen and phosphorus in the spring.

use a mulch, such as shredded bark, but in a scented garden you should seek out densely leaved ground-cover plants instead. These will shade the soil and block the light, as well as emit fragrance from their flowers and/or foliage if you choose the right variety, such as a low-growing rose (*Rosa*) or thyme (*Thymus*).

Dwarf shrubs such as this Daphne retusa *can be used as ground cover to help control weeds as well as provide fragrance.*

Windbreaks

The wind can be both cold and strong in spring, and delicate new leaves and shoots can be damaged by it. Both are at their most vulnerable in spring, before they have had a chance to toughen up, and a period of strong wind can cause extensive damage. The cells are chilled and dried, resulting in an effect known as scorching, because that is exactly what it resembles.

Use windbreaks to help make sure that tender young plants are kept sufficiently warm. These may be temporary or movable, such as plastic mesh, horticultural fleece, or a cloche, or permanent. The most permanent is a wall, but the danger of a solid barrier is that it diverts the wind upward, causing it to swirl. This turbulence can produce more damage to the plants on the other side of the wall than the wind would have done. A permeable material that allows some of the wind to filter through is more effective, such as plastic mesh, woven wooden fencing, willow hurdles, or living hedges. All of these will have a screening effect, giving privacy as well as less wind disturbance. In a small garden, a screening plant such as bamboo can be planted in a container with wheels, to be moved around the garden to the places where it is most useful at any particular time.

Propagation & planting

Spring is the busiest time of year for seed propagation, because this is the time when light levels begin to increase and temperatures rise. If you are planning a display of annual color and fragrance, it is important to sow the seeds now, because the young plants need to grow and mature in time to produce the flowers. With practice, it is possible to sow successive batches of seeds so that you get flowers throughout the summer, rather than in one brief display. Soft-tip cuttings can be taken from plants such as geranium (*Pelargonium*) in order to increase your stocks. Both seedlings and cuttings need repotting regularly to keep them growing strongly, and they need protection from inclement weather, which can kill the plants or encourage disease.

Seedlings and cuttings

Sow seeds at this time of year, aiming for a range of flowering times so that you have a strong display throughout the season. A greenhouse is ideal for this and can make both indoor and outdoor gardening easier. If you are planning a summer display, you can bulk up your plant numbers by taking cuttings from existing plants or new ones as they grow in the greenhouse.

If the greenhouse is heated, you can use it to protect any plants that will be affected by frost and to hurry plants along a little to reduce any gaps in the planned displays throughout the colder months of the year. If you do not have a greenhouse and are planting seeds in the open, cover them with individual or tunnel cloches overnight and during bad weather (see below).

Resting plants

While the new season's seedlings and cuttings are growing on a shelf in the greenhouse, use the space on the floor below to allow indoor plants to rest and recuperate after their displays have finished. Bulbs look less than attractive while their foliage dies down, but they need somewhere to replenish their energy and prepare for the next season, and a corner of a greenhouse or cold frame is ideal.

Planting out

After germination, seedlings need care to ensure they continue to grow and do not succumb to pests, disease, or the weather. If they are in trays or pots, you need to acclimatize them as they get bigger by exposing them to the elements during the day and returning them to a protected environment overnight until the weather is warm enough to leave them outside all the time. They may need overnight protection for some time, so do not be tempted by a few warm days and put them in their final planting position until all danger of late frost has passed.

Alternatively, place the seedlings in an unheated greenhouse or cold frame. This is warmer than outdoors but cooler than indoors, making it an ideal "halfway house" for acclimatizing plants. The drawback is that you could be caught off guard by a rogue frost and lose a valued plant. Once the seedlings have been successfully acclimatized, plant them out into a well-prepared plot so that they can continue growing to maturity.

You can take soft-tip cuttings from geraniums (Pelargonium) *during the spring. Repot the cuttings regularly to ensure strong growth.*

Spring is the busiest time of year for sowing seeds and nurturing young seedlings. The rewards in the summer will be well worth the effort.

Feeding young plants

You should incorporate a suitable feed into the ground as you plant out seedlings and cuttings, or apply a liquid fertilizer once the plants are growing strongly (this is particularly important if you are sowing seed directly into its final position). Liquid feeds are easy and convenient, because they can be applied when the plants are watered. Remember to do this regularly, because some is always washed away through the soil.

Sheltering young plants

The weather can have a profound effect on plant growth and a windbreak may be the difference between life and death for a young plant. If your garden is exposed, it makes sense to keep some protection on hand that can be put into place around the plants in the event of a period of bad weather. A temporary windbreak, such as netting around the immediate area, may be sufficient in spring when the young seedlings are planted out. If the garden is windswept throughout the year, it may be worth considering a permanent solution (see Windbreaks, page 53).

Using a cloche

A cloche is a small, often portable structure that can be placed over a plant to protect it from the weather. It may be plastic or glass and should allow the maximum amount of light to reach the plant. Cloches can also be used for night protection by placing the structure over the plant as the temperatures fall and removing it in the morning as they rise again. Protecting the plant encourages it to grow more quickly than its exposed counterparts, producing its flowers earlier and with less damage. Used on bare earth before planting, the cloche can warm the soil more quickly than if it were unprotected, allowing earlier planting. Plastic sheets can be used as a tunnel to cover a much larger area for planting a whole row.

Pruning

Some of the most fragrant plants produce their flowers at the most unlikely time of year. During the chilly winter season, a brief period of winter sunshine can produce a burst of blooms with a very strong fragrance. It is important that you prune these plants in spring immediately after flowering to ensure a strong display of flowers in future years.

WHAT YOU NEED
Tools: Pruning shears, pruning saw, garden fork

Plants such as the Standish's honeysuckle are capable of producing flowers from late autumn until late winter (*Lonicera standishii*) and midwinter until midspring (*L. fragrantissima* and *L.* x *purpusii*). These plants produce their flowering wood during the current growing season and very rarely flower on two-year-old wood. They must therefore be pruned to ensure a fresh supply of flowering shoots in years to come.

The best time to do this is in spring immediately after flowering, just as the old flowers are fading. By cutting off the growth that is carrying the fading flowers, you can be certain that the right shoots are being removed. This will create the space needed for future flowering wood. As the plant matures, some of the oldest stems will need to be removed completely to encourage a more open habit and to create space in the center of the shrub for new shoots to grow from the base. Each year, about a quarter of the oldest stems should be cut down to their base.

Tip: Some shrubs, such as *Daphne bholua*, *Jasminum nudiflorum*, *Mahonia* x *media*, *Sarcococca humilis*, *Viburnum* x *bodnantense*, and the honeysuckles mentioned above, naturally produce long branches that often arch over to touch the ground. They may begin to form roots where they touch the soil, producing new shrubs by a process known as "simple layering." It is important that you do not prune these shoots until the new plant has had the chance to develop a good root system.

Start by cutting out any dead, dying, diseased, or damaged stems using a pair of pruning shears. Then cut out those shoots that have old, fading flowers on them. Cut them back to a strong pair of buds close to the main stem.

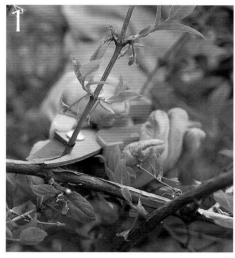

Remove about a quarter of the oldest shoots from the plant. Cut as close to ground level as possible. These are usually the thicker stems with darker colored bark. For the thickest, it is easier to use a pruning saw than pruning shears.

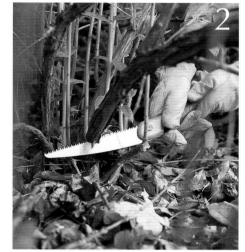

If possible, leave strong, young shoots growing from the center of the plant undamaged. These will become replacements for the older growth that is being removed.

Where shoots have arched over and rooted into the ground (simple layering), gently ease the roots out of the ground using a garden fork. These new plants can be transferred to sites in other parts of the garden if required.

Prune back any new shoots that are long and straggly by a third of their total length from the tip. Always prune to a pair of healthy buds, because this promotes rapid healing of the pruning cuts and reduces the chance of these shoots dying.

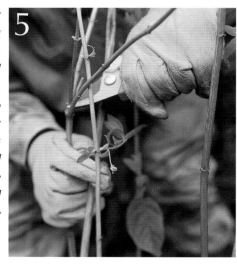

Any discarded branches and shoots should be taken away for shredding or disposal. Remove any small twigs or branches left lying on the ground around the plant to help prevent disease from spreading into the shrub.

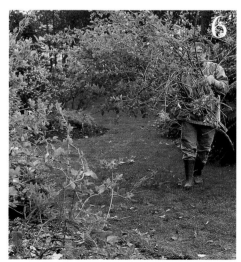

Fragrant ground cover

It is possible to have a fragrant garden that is also low-maintenance. Many of the more modern varieties of "ground-cover" roses have a low, spreading habit as well as scented blooms. This means that they will eventually form a dense leaf canopy, providing a living mulch of plants that will suppress many of the weeds encountered in the garden, as well as creating a fragrant carpet.

WHAT YOU NEED
Tools: Spade, knife, wheelbarrow, garden fork
Materials: Pot-grown roses, landscape fabric, organic mulch

For ground-cover plants to work effectively, their site must be well-prepared and free from all traces of perennial weeds. This will give the newly introduced plants the best possible start. Using ground-cover roses in conjunction with a mulch will give even more effective cover and can also be used for aesthetic effect. Planting roses through landscape fabric covered with a layer of dark brown bark nuggets or shredded wood fiber, for example, can set up a striking contrast between the different shades of green foliage and the texture of the mulch.

There are three main reasons for covering the fabric—weighing down the fabric will keep it from flapping in the wind, landscape fabric looks unsightly, and plastic biodegrades quickly when exposed to sunlight. The main purpose of the mulch is to control the weeds until the new plants become established, and to reduce the need for watering by trapping moisture in the soil and preventing water loss through evaporation from the soil surface. Usually, the only maintenance required is to keep deadheading the roses to ensure that a continuous supply of sweetly scented flowers is produced throughout the growing season.

> **Tip:** Lightly trim ground-cover roses with a hedge trimmer immediately after flowering. You should remove around the top third of the growth. This will encourage another flush of flowers.

Start by marking out where each plant is going to be positioned, or stand the plants (in their containers) in their intended positions. This will give a better idea of how the bed will look when it has been planted.

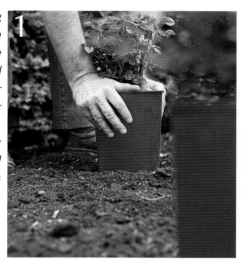

Remove the plants and dig a planting hole large enough to accommodate the whole root system, keeping the topsoil and subsoil separate. Spread the subsoil over the surface of the bed and keep the topsoil close to the planting hole.

Place a sheet of heavy-gauge landscape fabric over the bed and seal the edges by tucking them in, at least 6 in. deep, and stretching the fabric as tightly as possible.

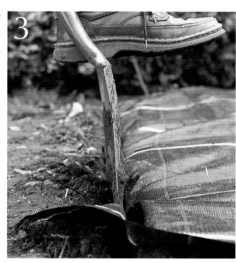

Press down gently onto the fabric to find the location of the planting holes, and cut a cross in the fabric at the point where each plant is to be placed.

Fold back the flaps of the cross to reveal the planting hole beneath. Holding the plant by its stem or leaves, gently remove it from the container. Position the plant in the planting hole, pull the soil back into the hole around the plant, and firm gently into place.

Immediately after planting, fold the plastic flaps back into position around the base of the plant. Hide the fabric by covering it with a layer of organic material such as bark chips or wood chips, and spread it evenly over the fabric.

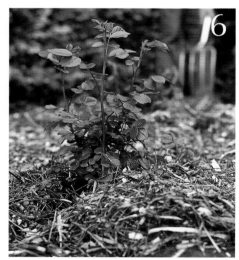

Fragrance indoors

The first few weeks of spring can seem dull in the garden, with leafless trees taking on a gray cast and grass turning a drab gray-green. Even if your garden has color and interest in the late winter and early spring, the weather may be too cold for you to spend much time outside appreciating it. Therefore, this is a good time to ensure that you have plenty of color and fragrance indoors. This will cheer you up and remind you that the warmer days of late spring and summer really are just around the corner.

Bulbs

One of the easiest ways to create indoor color is with bulbs, which can be chosen to flower in succession from midwinter until late spring. Bulbs are small, conveniently packaged, and not overly demanding of attention. In return for compost and regular watering, they provide colorful flowers that fill the house with natural fragrance. You can choose the color and amount of fragrance they release to suit you and your home. Miniature *Narcissus* such as 'Tête-à-Tête' reach about 8 in. high and have a sweet, delicate perfume. Taller varieties such as 'Paper White' (*N. papyraceus*) reach 18 in., and their scent is powerful. Hyacinths (*Hyacinthus*) are highly scented and may need a stake for support as they open, because the weight of the flower may pull the stem over.

Bulbs take ten to twelve weeks to develop and flower, so plant them in the fall to provide color for early spring. Choose an attractive container and plant them in bulb compost. Keep the compost thoroughly moist but not wet. Once the flowers begin to open, apply a general liquid fertilizer every two weeks when you are watering. As the flowers die, remove them to keep the plant from wasting energy by setting seeds. Leave the flower stem intact so that it and the leaves can die down naturally and replenish the bulb for the following year. Continue watering and feeding until the foliage has died completely back, then let the bulb dry out. Store it until the following year or plant it in the garden to provide color for years to come.

Growing conditions

All bulbs and indoor plants have a range of conditions in which they will thrive, and another in which they can survive. Different parts of the house offer very different conditions, and the levels of light, heat, and humidity vary considerably. Plants share a common dislike of drafts and extremes of temperature, but otherwise have different growing requirements.

Light

Light levels are important, and they drop quickly as you move away from the window. Plants with white- or yellow-variegated leaves need the highest levels, and those with dark green leaves can tolerate the deepest shade. By selecting the variety to suit the position, it is possible to find a plant for all but the darkest corner.

If the weather is still too cold in spring to spend much time in the garden, bring cut flowers into the home to enjoy their fragrance.

Narcissus are available in many different forms, from extravagant double-flowered varieties to simple trumpet-shaped blooms. Plant bulbs of different varieties that will flower in succession throughout the spring.

Heat

Plants that prefer warm conditions, such as *Gardenia* and *Hoya*, are ideal for kitchens and bathrooms, whereas those needing a cooler environment, such as *Jasminum* and *Stephanotis*, may suit the bedroom. If the plant is on the windowsill during winter, move it into the main part of the room overnight, because the temperature behind closed curtains can be 18°F colder than inside, and the plant can suffer cold damage if it is left there.

Humidity

Humidity can be increased around plants such as *Citrus* and *Gardenia* by standing the pot on a saucer of gravel and water. The water will evaporate up the pot, creating moist conditions around the leaves. Grouping plants together helps to trap this moisture and create a microenvironment. The roots of the plant must not be allowed to stand in the water or they will rot.

Sunrooms

A sunroom offers many possibilities for growing plants, with extra space and high light levels. Many indoor plants thrive in these conditions, like the strongly fragrant white jasmine (*Jasminum polyanthum*), which is tolerant of cooler temperatures. Other plants may not survive over winter unless the sunroom is heated, including aromatic plants such as *Citrus* (oranges and lemons). These are ideal for large sunrooms, where their aromatic foliage can provide respite from the sun.

Forcing bulbs

Many of the hardy bulbs that bloom outdoors during late winter and spring can be tempted into flowering indoors many weeks earlier by using specially prepared bulbs. These bulbs are known as "forced" bulbs, and they can provide an excellent display of indoor color and fragrance during the colder months, when gardening outdoors may be difficult.

WHAT YOU NEED

Materials: Compost; plant pots; bulbs; straw, newspaper, or sand; bulb bowls; grit or sphagnum moss; high-potassium fertilizer; stakes and string (for tall-stemmed flowers)

Forced bulbs have been given special treatment to advance their development and shorten their growing season. This involves the gardener lifting the bulbs from the field and storing them for a period of time in storage sheds at temperatures of 77–95°F to speed up the development of the flower bud. The second stage of treatment is a period of about six weeks' storage at a much lower temperature, usually below 50°F. This is done to mimic the winter cold that the bulbs would experience naturally so that they will start into growth earlier than normal. All of this preparation is carried out before the bulbs are offered for sale in garden centers and stores.

Hyacinths have been used in this project. However, the difficulty with forcing hyacinths of mixed colors is that no two cultivars grow at exactly the same rate, and there is nothing more disappointing than having the flowers open at different times rather than simultaneously. To combat this problem, grow each color separately so that you can slow down or advance its development to keep the growth of each batch balanced with the others. Plant the bulbs for forcing in late summer or early autumn, keeping bulbs of the same cultivar together.

Tip: Keep the bulbs well watered to maintain a good show of flowers. After flowering, remove the flower head (but leave the green flower stem) and put the bowl in a cool place. Continue to feed and water the bulbs until they are ready to be planted outdoors in April.

Sprinkle a layer of compost in the bottom of the pot and insert the bulb; make sure it does not touch the sides of the pot. Fill in the spaces between the pot rim and the bulb with compost, and firm it gently so that it is ½ in. below the rim of the container to allow for watering.

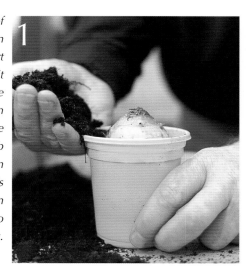

Immediately after potting your bulbs, you need to give them a cold period for eight to ten weeks. This can be achieved by placing them in a cool garage or dry shed, covered with moist straw, sand, or shredded newspaper.

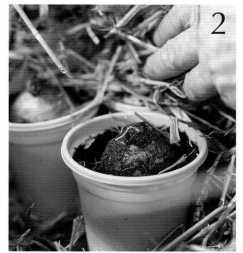

Alternatively, place the pots of bulbs in a cold frame. Cover with straw, sand, or shredded newspaper and wet them thoroughly (this is known as "plunging"). Keeping the bulbs moist helps to lower the temperature.

When the flower spike is about 2 in. high, bring the pots indoors and place them in a cool, shaded place at 50°F for about a week, during which time the shoots will turn green.

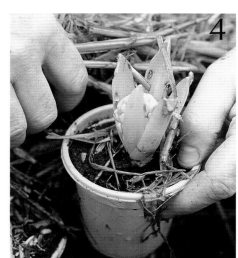

Knock the individual bulbs out of their pots and plant them into bulb bowls. Place a layer of grit or sphagnum moss over the surface of the compost to hold in the moisture. Feed the bulbs every seven days with a high-potassium fertilizer.

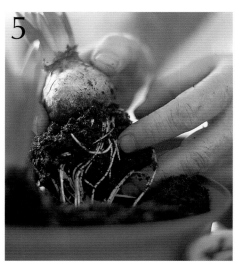

Keep the bowls in a well-lit position at a temperature of 59–63°F. Turn the bowls every day so that bulbs grow evenly and do not lean toward the light. Tie the flower stems of taller cultivars to stakes if they need support.

TREES

Acacia longifolia
H 46 ft. S 26 ft.
Sun
Moderate
Acid/neutral Z8

This Australian native, commonly called the Sydney golden wattle, grows to become a small tree or large evergreen shrub with an open habit. The mid-green flattened, modified leaves (called *phyllodes*) are straplike or lance-shaped, reaching up to 6 in. long with a slender, curved tip. In spring, fragrant, deep-yellow, cylindrical flower heads up to 3 in. long and ½ in. across are produced on anything from one to three spikes. Acacias resent severe pruning and will often die back. Propagate by sowing seeds into pots and placing them in a heated case in spring or by taking semiripe tip cuttings in summer.

Laburnum x ***watereri* 'Vossii'**
H 32 ft. S 26 ft.
Sun
Moderate
Any Z6

The golden chain tree is a popular deciduous flowering tree with a slightly erect habit and gray-green branches. The gray-green leaves are made up of three small, oval-shaped leaflets that are glossy on the upper surface and paler on the underside. During spring, large quantities of long, hanging clusters of golden yellow, pealike flowers with a faint scent of freesia are produced. These are followed by small, gray-brown pods that disperse poisonous black seeds in the fall. This plant will grow in a wide range of soils but has a brittle root system and must be permanently staked. Propagate by budding or grafting.

Magnolia kobus
H 39 ft. S 32 ft.
Sun/partial shade
Moderate/moist
Any Z5

A native of Japan, this is an early
flowering deciduous magnolia that
develops into a broadly conical-
shaped tree. The aromatic leaves
are oval in shape and a mid-green
color, sometimes with a puckered
edge when they first emerge.
In early spring, the tree becomes
covered in large, strongly scented,
goblet-shaped blooms that open
to form a "cup and saucer"-shaped
flower. They are white and
sometimes flushed with pink at the
base of each petal. Propagate by
layering in spring, taking semiripe
cuttings in summer, or sowing seed
as soon as it is ripe.

Magnolia x soulangeana
H 23 ft. S 20 ft.
Sun/partial shade
Moderate
Acid/neutral Z5

This beautiful deciduous hybrid
magnolia grows to form an
architectural, wide-spreading tree.
In spring, it becomes covered in
large goblet-shaped blooms that
resemble a water lily flower when
they are fully open. They may be
white or light pink through darker
shades of pink to violet-purple,
and are lightly lemon-scented.
The leaves, which appear as the
flowers die off, are elliptical in
shape and a glossy dark green in
color, sometimes lightly tinted with
bronze when they are young. The
cultivar 'Alba Superba' has strongly
scented flowers. Propagate by
layering in spring.

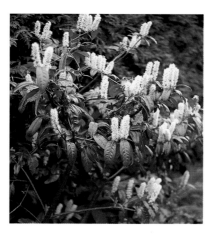

Prunus laurocerasus
H 26 ft. S 32 ft.
Sun
Moderate
Any Z7

Commonly called the cherry laurel,
this dense, bushy small tree or large
shrub forms into a framework of
arching, spreading branches. It has
evergreen elliptical leaves that are
a glossy dark green above and paler
on the underside. It is a relative of
the cherry and is much valued for
its profusion of spring flowers,
which are creamy white and
heavily scented, appearing on spikes
through the canopy of evergreen
leaves. The flowers are followed by
red, cherrylike fruits that turn black
as they become fully ripe. Propagate
by taking semiripe heel cuttings in
summer and fall.

SHRUBS

Corylopsis sinensis
H 12 ft. S 12 ft.
Partial shade
Moderate
Acid/neutral Z6

This beautiful, deciduous flowering shrub has slender stems and a dense, branching habit. In spring, it produces drooping strands of lemon-yellow flowers, which are highly fragrant and appear before the leaves have opened. The leaves are broadly-oval shaped with bristle-like teeth along the margins. When they appear, the new leaves are dark-green on their upper surface and bluish-green underneath. The delicate flowers may be damaged by late spring frosts. Propagate by taking softwood cuttings in summer or by sowing seed in a cold frame in the autumn.

Cytisus x kewensis
H 2 ft. S 5 ft.
Sun
Moderate
Any Z6

Raised at London's Kew Gardens in 1891, this low-growing, sprawling deciduous shrub has remained popular ever since. In spring, cascades of sweetly scented, creamy yellow, sweet pea–shaped blooms are produced that cover the entire bush and obscure the stems and leaves. The mid-green leaves are small, straplike, and covered with very fine hairs. This plant does not respond well to being moved and being pruned vigorously. Propagate by taking semiripe heel cuttings in summer.

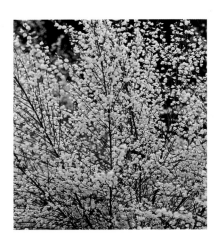

Cytisus multiflorus
H 10 ft. S 8 ft.
Sun
Moderate
Any Z6

Commonly known as the white Spanish broom, this attractive sprawling deciduous shrub grows upright at first before developing an open, spreading habit. In spring, it is covered with creamy white, sweet pea–shaped blooms that have a sweet fragrance. The straplike leaves are mid-green in color and sparsely arranged along the thin, lax, twiggy green stems. It does not respond well to being moved or to hard pruning. Propagate by taking semiripe heel cuttings in summer.

SHRUBS

Daphne mezereum
H 4 ft. S 3 ft.
Sun/partial shade
Moderate
Neutral Z4

Originating from Europe and central
Asia, this slow-growing deciduous
shrub has an upright habit and dull,
pale green to gray-green leaves that
are about 5 in. long. It produces a
spectacular display of intensely
fragrant flowers in late winter and
early spring, long before the leaves
emerge. The flowers are pinkish-
purple, up to ¼ in. long and carried
in clusters of two to five blooms,
followed by spherical, fleshy red
fruits. Prune only to remove dead
or damaged wood and move as
little as possible because it does
not respond well to being
disturbed. Propagate by taking
semiripe cuttings in summer.

Euphorbia mellifera
H 7 ft. S 8 ft.
Sun
Well-drained/moderate
Any Z10

Originating from Madeira and
commonly called the honey spurge,
this rounded evergreen shrub has
stout stems and dark green, straplike
leaves up to 8 in. long, with a
prominent rib along the center. In
late spring, an assembly of large
brown bracts (modified leaves often
mistaken for flowers) are carried on
the tip of each stem and produce a
strong scent of honey. These are
followed by pealike fruits in late
summer. Propagate by sowing seeds
in a cold frame as soon as it is ripe
or by taking semiripe tip cuttings
in late spring or early summer.

Mahonia aquifolium
H 4 ft. S 4 ft.
Sun/partial shade
Moderate
Any Z5

Commonly known as the Oregon
grape, this tough evergreen shrub
has a spreading, suckering habit
and is useful as ground cover or
under trees in a woodland garden.
The glossy, dark green leaves are
divided into up to nine leaflets
that have bright crimson edges in
winter. In spring, sweetly scented
yellow flowers are produced in
dense clusters on the shoot tips.
Attractive cultivars include *M. a.*
'Atropurpurea' (rich red-purple
leaves in winter) and *M. a.* 'Apollo'
(low growing with golden yellow
flowers). Prune only to maintain
the shape and health of the plant.
Propagate by taking semiripe
cuttings in late summer or suckers
in autumn.

SHRUBS

Osmanthus x burkwoodii
H 10 ft. S 10 ft.
Sun/partial shade
Moderate
Any Z6

This plant is a hybrid between
O. decorus and O. delavayi.
It is a slow-growing evergreen shrub
with a dense, rounded habit, often
spreading with age. The glossy,
dark green leaves have a leathery
texture and are broadly elliptical
in shape, about 2 in. long, with a
slightly toothed margin. In mid- to
late spring, small, tubular, fragrant
flowers are produced in small
clusters in the axils of the leaves
and stem, but being a hybrid plant,
it very rarely produces fruits.
Propagate by sowing seeds in a cold
frame as soon as it is ripe or by
taking semiripe cuttings in summer.

Osmanthus delavayi
H 7 ft. S 7 ft.
Sun/partial shade
Moderate
Any Z7

This rounded evergreen shrub has
arching branches and is ideal for
a border. The leathery, dark green
leaves have toothed edges and
remain glossy throughout the year.
In late spring, the strongly fragrant
white flowers appear in clusters
along the shoots, each tubular in
shape, flaring out into four lobes.
The flowers are followed by blue-
black fruits. If necessary, prune after
flowering to remove dead or
damaged wood, although it will
tolerate hard pruning and may be
trained against a wall. Propagate
by taking semiripe cuttings in late
summer or sowing seed as soon as
it is ripe.

Rhododendron cubittii
H 5 ft. S 3 ft.
Partial shade
Moderate
Acid Z10

Originating from northern Myanmar,
this suckering evergreen shrub is
still known by many gardeners as
an azalea. In winter, it produces
purple-brown young shoots. In
spring, it produces large quantities
of highly fragrant white to pale pink
funnel-shaped blooms. These have
deep-orange or yellow markings and
form into a rounded truss. The mid-
to dark green, broadly oval-shaped
leaves are up to 4 in. long and have
a leathery texture. Propagate by
taking softwood cuttings in early
summer or sowing seed under
protection in late spring.

Rhododendron luteum
H 8 ft. S 10 ft.
Sun
Moderate
Acid/neutral Z5

This deciduous shrub is one of
the few scented rhododendrons
and one of the easiest to grow,
although it does prefer acidic soil.
In late spring, the large flower buds
open into long-tubed flowers that
are clear yellow and highly fragrant.
The leaves are broadly spear-
shaped, mid-green, and slightly
sticky when young, changing to
shades of crimson, purple, and
orange in autumn. Although quick
to establish, this plant will grow
slowly and steadily to form a large
dome shape. Propagate by taking
semiripe cuttings or by layering
in late summer.

Syringa oblata
H 16 ft. S 16 ft.
Sun
Moderate
Any Z7

Originating from Korea, this
vigorous shrub has an erect habit
when young, changing to an open,
spreading habit with age. The
deciduous heart-shaped leaves are
tapered to a point and tinted bronze
when young, changing to a glossy
mid-green as they mature and
turning purple before falling in
autumn. In mid- to late spring,
broad spikes of highly fragrant pale
lilac flowers are produced. The only
pruning required is removal of the
dead flowers. Propagate by taking
softwood cuttings or by layering
in early summer, by budding in
midsummer, or by grafting in winter.

Viburnum carlesii
H 7 ft. S 7 ft.
Sun/partial shade
Moderate
Any Z9

This slow-growing, densely twiggy
deciduous shrub is grown for its
beautiful, sweetly fragrant spring
flowers. These are produced before
the foliage in domed clusters at the
tips of the shoots. They are rose pink
in bud, opening to white-flushed
pink, and are followed by fruit that
ripens from red to black. The leaves
are coarse, toothed, and mid-green
and often turn red before falling in
autumn. The cultivar 'Aurora' has
deep-pink buds and pink flowers,
fading to white. This is a lovely
specimen for a border or container.
Prune lightly after flowering to
maintain the shape and remove
any damaged wood. Propagate by
taking soft-tip cuttings in summer.

CLIMBERS & WALL SHRUBS

Akebia quinata
H 16 ft. S 16 ft.
Sun/partial shade
Moderate
Any Z5

Known as the chocolate vine, this
is a semievergreen twining climber
with palmate leaves of mid-green,
tinted bronze as they emerge. The
vanilla-scented flowers appear in
spring, in rich maroon to chocolate
brown—hence the common name.
Male and female flowers are borne
within the same cluster; small
male ones at the tip and larger
female ones at the base. Long,
purple, sausage-shaped fruits will
be produced in a hot summer if
there is a second plant nearby to
pollinate. If necessary, prune after
flowering to maintain the shape.
Propagate by layering in spring,
taking semiripe cuttings in summer,
or sowing seed as soon as it is ripe.

Azara dentata
H 10 ft. S 10 ft.
Sun
Well-drained/moderate
Any Z8

Originating from Chile, this
evergreen shrub is a perfect choice
for growing against a hot, sunny
wall or in a sheltered garden. It
has slender, arching branches and
oval-shaped, glossy, dark green
leaves with a finely toothed margin,
often hairy on the underside. In
mid- to late spring, dense clusters
of deep-yellow, sweetly scented
flowers up to 2 in. across are
produced. Prune immediately after
flowering by cutting the flower-
bearing shoots back to four or five
buds. Propagate by taking semiripe
cuttings from the new side shoots
in mid- to late summer.

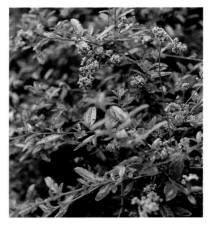

Ceanothus 'Cascade'
H 13 ft. S 13 ft.
Sun
Well-drained/moderate
Acid/neutral Z8

This vigorous, marginally hardy
evergreen shrub has an open,
wide-spreading habit. The glossy,
dark green leaves have a finely
toothed margin and are oblong to
oval in shape. The fragrant, soft
blue flowers are carried in large
pyramidal spikes up to 5 in. long
on the tips of the branches from
late spring until early summer. This
plant should be pruned immediately
after flowering to keep it from
becoming straggly and bare in the
center. It is often grown against a
wall to protect it from frost damage.
Propagate by taking semiripe
cuttings from the new side shoots
in mid- to late summer.

CLIMBERS & WALL SHRUBS

Clematis armandii
H 13 ft. S 10 ft.
Sun
Moderate
Any Z6

This attractive woody climber is
one of the few evergreen clematises.
It is ideal against a wall or fence
because it needs shade over its
roots. The glossy, leathery, trifoliate
leaves are up to 6 in. long and tend
to be tinted bronze as they emerge,
aging to a rich, dark green. In early
spring, fragrant, saucer-shaped,
pink-tinted, white flowers are
produced in dense clusters. 'Apple
Blossom' has a darker shading of
pink on the flowers, and 'Snowdrift'
is pure white. After flowering, prune
back to a strong pair of buds to
encourage flowering wood for the
following year. Propagate by taking
semiripe cuttings in late summer.

Lonicera syringantha
H 7 ft. S 8 ft.
Sun/shade
Moderate
Any Z4

This spring-flowering shrubby
honeysuckle is grown for its fragrant
flowers, which are arranged in pairs
and usually carried in small clusters
in the leaf joints of the branches.
The flowers are basically tubular
in shape, opening out to a broad
mouth, and are lilac-pink in color,
often paler inside. The deciduous
leaves are broadly oblong in shape
and gray-green to deep green in
color. They are carried in pairs
on thin, twiggy stems, gradually
developing an open, spreading
habit. Propagate by taking
hardwood cuttings of nonflowering
shoots in winter or softwood
cuttings in midsummer.

Wisteria sinensis
H 32 ft. S 32 ft.
Sun/partial shade
Moderate
Any Z5

This wisteria is a beautiful, elegant
climbing plant, especially when
draped with its cascades of fragrant,
pealike, white, pink, blue, or mauve
flowers. These appear in late spring
on the bare branches, before the
leaves emerge. The leaves are dark
to mid-green in color and divided
into small leaflets, and the plant
grows best in a south- or west-
facing situation. The vigorous stems
will twine in a counterclockwise
direction up a trellis or other
support. The white-flowered *W. s.*
'Alba' and the white-tinged purple
flowers of *W. s.* 'Sierra Madre' are
among the most fragrant. Propagate
by layering, grafting, or taking
softwood cuttings in summer.

PERENNIALS & BIENNIALS

Asphodeline lutea
H 5 ft. S 12 in.
Sun
Well-drained/moderate
Neutral Z7

Commonly known as the king's spear, this clump-forming perennial plant has long, narrow, straplike leaves that are deeply grooved, bluish-green in color, and produced along the length of the main stem and flower spike. In late spring and early summer, dense, tightly packed spikes of flowers up to 8 in. long are produced. They carry large numbers of fragrant, star-shaped, bright yellow flowers that open progressively from the base of the spike up to the tip. Propagate by sowing seeds into pots as soon as they are ripe and placing them in a cold frame, or by dividing in late summer or early autumn.

Erysimum cheiri
H 2 ft. S 2 ft.
Sun
Moderate
Alkaline/neutral Z7

This wallflower is an evergreen shrub with woody stems that form a low mound or dome of leaves. The straplike leaves are dark green with a slightly paler underside and are arranged in opposite pairs on gray-green stems. In early spring, the flowers are carried above the leaves in dense spikes of flat, four-petaled flowers. The cultivar 'Harpur Crewe' has fragrant, double, mustard-yellow flowers and will last about five years before it will need to be replaced. 'Bowles Mauve' has small, rich mauve blooms and silver-gray leaves. Propagate by taking softwood cuttings in late spring after flowering.

Myosotis sylvatica
H 12 in. S 6 in.
Sun/partial shade
Moderate
Any Z5

The woodland forget-me-not is a pretty, if invasive, biennial that grows from seeds sown one summer to flower the following spring. It self-seeds easily and is ideal for mixed borders or wooded areas where it can spread. In a container, remove the seed heads before any seeds are shed. The tiny, fragrant flowers are blue, occasionally pink or white, with a yellow or white eye. They are borne on tall spikes with a curled top that unfurls as the flowers open from the base upward over a period of several weeks. The smaller, compact forms, such as 'Blue Ball' and 'Snowball' (white), are suitable as spring bedding.

Primula
H 8 in. S 8 in.
Sun/partial shade
Moderate
Any Z6

This large genus of plants includes auricula, English primrose, and polyanthus. All have a basal rosette of rough leaves and wide-flaring, funnel-shaped, fragrant flowers. They are grouped according to botanical characteristics. *P. auricula* (auricula) has flowers in a cluster on a stout stem above the foliage in deep yellow, red, or purple with a yellow center. *P. vulgaris* (English primrose) bears solitary, pale yellow flowers on short, slender stems amid the foliage. *P. polyantha* (polyanthus) hybrids have primrose-shaped flowers in clusters on a stem above the foliage in maroon, red, orange, yellow, pink, white, or blue. Propagate by sowing seeds in spring or dividing in autumn.

Smilacina stellata
H 20 in. S 18 in.
Partial shade
Moderate/moist
Any Z3

A native of North America and Mexico and commonly known as the starflower, this clump-forming, hardy herbaceous perennial has long, narrow, lance-shaped mid-green leaves, slightly hairy on the underside, emerging from a creeping horizontal stem. From late spring into summer, small spikes of white, sweetly scented, star-shaped flowers are produced to form arching sprays on slender green stems. This plant must be sheltered from cold winds. Propagate by sowing seeds in spring or autumn or by dividing as soon as flowering has finished.

Viola cornuta
H 6 in. S 16 in.
Sun/partial shade
Moderate
Any Z7

The stems of this spreading evergreen perennial violet are flat at first and then turn upward. It has glossy, oval-shaped leaves with toothed edges and lightly fragrant flowers during spring and early summer. These are about 1½ in. across with five widely separate petals of lilac to violet. The lower petals have white markings and thin, slightly curved spurs. White, yellow, pink, and red forms have been bred. Ideally, it should be positioned under other plants in a border or in a permanent container. Propagate by sowing seeds in spring as soon as it is ripe or by dividing established clumps in spring (after flowering) or fall.

BULBS, CORMS, & RHIZOMES

Convallaria majalis
H 9 in. S 12 in.
Partial shade/shade
Moderate/moist
Any Z3

The lily of the valley is a beautiful
rhizomatous perennial that will
thrive in a shady spot beneath
other plants or in a container.
It is low growing and spreads as
ground cover. Pots of them can
be brought indoors to a cool room
or sunroom for flowering, where
the sweet fragrance can be fully
appreciated. Broad, oval, basal
leaves surround an upright,
flowering stalk bearing pretty,
hanging, bell-shaped white flowers
in spring. The cultivar 'Albostriata'
has white-striped leaves, 'Flore
Pleno' has double flowers, and
var. *rosea* has pale pink flowers.
Propagate by dividing the rhizomes
in autumn, but do not allow them
to dry out.

Freesia
H 18 in. S 2 in.
Sun
Moderate
Any Z9

Although freesias are commonly
found as cut flowers in florist
shops, they are easy to grow from
dry corms and provide a long-
lasting display. The beautiful long,
funnel-shaped flowers are highly
fragrant, held on arching stems, and
come in a wide range of colors,
including red, orange, pink, white,
blue, lilac, and yellow. Double-
flowered forms are available,
although they are not generally
as fragrant as the single blooms.
The leaves are long, thin, and lance-
shaped, bright green, and arranged
in a flat fan shape. Propagate by
sowing seed or offsets in a
greenhouse or indoors in autumn.

Hyacinthus orientalis
H 8–12 in. S 3 in.
Sun/partial shade
Moderate
Any Z6

Hyacinths are bulbous perennials
with colorful and highly scented
waxy flowers. These are bell-shaped,
single or double, and come in
shades of white, yellow, pink,
orange, red, and blue in clusters
of up to forty on a single broad,
upright stem amid bright green,
straplike leaves. 'Blue Jacket' (single,
navy blue), 'City of Haarlem'
(single, primrose yellow), 'Delft
Blue' (single, powder blue), 'Gipsy
Queen' (single, orange-pink),
'Hollyhock' (double, crimson),
and 'L'innocence' (single, white)
are just some of the colors available.
Propagate by removing small offsets
in summer when the bulb is
dormant. Plant with the tip of the
bulb 1 in. below the surface of the
soil in autumn.

BULBS, CORMS, & RHIZOMES

Iris unguicularis
H 18 in. S 2 in.
Sun/partial shade
Moderate
Alkaline/neutral Z5

This tough evergreen plant has dark green, broadly straplike leaves up to 2 ft. in length. The primrose-scented flowers consist of delicate, silky petals, colored lilac with a yellow center, and carried on short stems from late autumn to early spring. There are two very good cultivars: *I. u.* 'Mary Barnard,' which has deep violet-blue flowers with dark veins, and the free-flowering *I. u.* 'Walter Butt,' which has pale, silvery lavender flowers. Propagate by dividing established plants immediately after flowering.

Narcissus
H 4–24 in. S 2–6 in.
Sun/partial shade
Moderate
Any Z6

There are hundreds of varieties of these hardy perennial spring-flowering bulbs. They have narrow, straplike leaves and flowers with an inner trumpet or cup and an outer row of petals. Flower shades include yellow, white, orange, cream, and pink. They may be single or clustered, with single or double petals, and of varying lengths and shapes of trumpet. They range from 4-in. dwarf types to tall, 2-ft. varieties. Deadhead after flowering to keep energy from being expended on seed formation and remove brown foliage during midsummer. Plant the dormant bulbs at one-and-a-half times their own depth in autumn. Lift and divide every three to five years, six weeks after flowering.

Tulipa
H 8–20 in. S 4in.
Sun
Moderate
Any Z5

Tulips are perennial spring-flowering bulbs, classified according to botanical characteristics and time of flowering. The flowers may be single, double, goblet- or star-shaped, fringed, or long and slender. Flower shades include white, yellow, pink, red, orange, and purple to almost black.
T. kaufmanniana hybrids (water lily tulips)—'Giuseppe Verdi' (yellow and red striped flowers) and *T. greigii* 'Red Riding Hood' (red flowers), for example—are low growing. *T. praestans* bears clusters of up to five orange-red flowers. Deadhead after flowering and allow to die down. Plant new bulbs in autumn 4–6 in. deep. Propagate by dividing when the bulbs are lifted after flowering.

INDOOR PLANTS

Citrus limon
H 7 ft. S 5 ft.
Sun
Moderate

Citrus plants are ideal for
the house or sunroom, where
they produce flowers and fruit
intermittently throughout the year
when conditions are warm enough.
The stems are spiny and the glossy,
deep-green leaves are oval shaped.
The fragrant, purple-tinged white
flowers have five blunt petals and
large stamens. Each fruit ripens from
green to yellow, so that there will
be fruit of each color on the plant
at the same time. How palatable
they are depends on the variety.
C. l. 'Variegata' has leaves that are
variegated cream and fruit that are
striped green, becoming fully yellow
as they mature. Propagate by taking
semiripe tip heel cuttings in spring
or summer.

Gardenia augusta
H 18 in. S 18 in.
Partial shade
Moderate

This bushy evergreen shrub is
grown for its large, waxy flowers,
which are up to 3 in. across, white,
and intensely fragrant. They are
usually double (many-petaled) but
also occur as semidouble (two
layers of petals). The lance-shaped,
dark green leaves are 2–4 in. long,
glossy, and leathery. It prefers to
grow in conditions of warmth and
high humidity, especially while
the flower buds are forming, so
stand the pot on a tray of moist
pebbles and mist the plant
frequently. Any pruning should
be done immediately after
flowering, removing faded flowers
and cutting back to an outward-
facing bud. Propagate by taking
tip cuttings in spring.

Genista falcata
H 3 ft. S 5 ft.
Sun
Well-drained/moderate

Originating from Spain and
Portugal, this small, deciduous
gorselike shrub is erect when
young but develops a rounded,
low-spreading habit with slender,
drooping, green branches. The
branches are almost leafless, with
many of the side shoots ending
with sharp spines at the tips. The
tough, sparse leaves are mid-green
in color and straplike, with fine
white, silky hairs produced only
on the youngest shoots. The heavily
scented, pealike flowers are deep
golden yellow and produced in
large quantities on the tips of shoots
in mid- and late spring. Propagate
by sowing seeds in spring.

Hoya carnosa
H 16 ft. S 7 ft.
Sun
Moderate

The miniature wax flower has trailing thick, fleshy leaves and fragrant flowers. It looks attractive in a hanging basket, where the scent and the detail of the flowers can be appreciated. The stems are initially upright, arching only as they grow longer, and the dull green leaves are borne in pairs. The small flowers are deliciously fragrant and appear in clusters of up to ten at the ends of the shoots. Each is star-shaped, with waxy, white outer petals and a purple-red center. It likes bright, indirect light but dislikes being repotted or disturbed. Propagate by taking tip cuttings in spring or summer.

Murraya paniculata
H 16 ft. S 10 ft.
Sun
Moderate

This native of Southeast Asia, known as the orange jasmine or Chinese box, will ultimately grow to form a large, strongly aromatic evergreen tree or shrub, ideal for a sunroom. The dark green leaves are glossy, smooth, and divided into three or more oblong leaflets, each up to 2 in. long. The small, fragrant white flowers are produced in densely packed terminal clusters throughout the year and are followed by oval, orange-red fruit that are attractive but not edible. Propagate by sowing seeds in spring or taking semiripe tip cuttings in summer.

Stephanotis floribunda
H 10 ft. S 10 ft.
Sun
Moderate

The Madagascar jasmine is a climbing shrub best known for its heavily scented, waxy white flowers, but it also has wonderful leathery leaves of a glossy dark green. The 1-in.-long flowers are borne in clusters of ten or more, each tubular in shape and flaring out into five lobes. It needs support as it grows, and it will look equally attractive trained against a wall in a sunroom, or indoors on a small trellis or over an archway, as long as it is positioned where its fragrance can be fully appreciated. Pinch off the growing tips to encourage bushy growth. Propagate by taking tip cuttings in late spring.

chapter four

4

Plants for summer

Summer is the time to make the most of your garden and enjoy the fragrance that lingers in the warm air. Long days and warm evenings are ideal for enjoying a relaxing outdoor meal and appreciating the sights, sounds, and, above all, the scent of the great outdoors. By now, established plants should be growing well and young annual seedlings should be in their final growing positions, ready to give a burst of color as soon as they are mature. Many plants are at their best in the warm months of summer, in all shapes and sizes, from trees right down to ground cover. Their scents are as varied as the colors of their flowers, with some being noticeably strong and others much more subtle.

Roses

The rose is one of the most popular garden plants in cultivation. Species originating from countries as diverse as China, India, and France have been grown and bred over the years into the vast range of cultivars available today. Roses have long been prized for their distinctive perfume, and most of the rose species we grow today have retained their fragrance. However, many of the hybrids have lost some of their scent in the effort to produce a better flower. Roses fall into one of several categories, depending on their growth habit and type of flower. Because these range in size from tiny miniatures to very large shrubs, there is a rose suitable for every size of garden or for an attractive container.

- **Miniature roses**
  These come in many colors, with flowers varying from single to fully double. Their size makes them ideal for containers, but they tend to lack a strong fragrance.

- **Patio roses**
  This type of rose is a recent introduction consisting of a miniature variety grafted onto a straight stem up to 3 ft. high. It is ideal for container growing.

- **Hybrid tea roses**
  These grow as bushes and have the largest flowers, usually double or semidouble, in colors ranging from blood-red through shades of pink, orange, and yellow to white. When pruned regularly, they will flower throughout the summer, especially if the heads are removed as they fade.

- **Multiflora (floribunda) roses**
  This type of rose produces blooms that are similar to those of hybrid tea roses, but usually smaller and in greater profusion. Multiflora roses come in a wide range of colors and will flower throughout the summer as long as they are deadheaded.

- **Shrub (species) roses**
  Shrub roses are varied, ranging from the 3-ft., intensely spiny *Rosa rugosa* group with strongly scented single, semidouble, or double flowers to large shrubs of 10 ft. such as the single-flowered *Rosa glauca*. Highly fragrant

Rosa 'Brother Cadfael' is one of the modern shrub roses that has been bred to combine strong fragrance with improved resistance to disease.

varieties include *Rosa mundi* (*R. gallica* 'Versicolor'), with its dramatic pink- and white-striped petals. These roses have one main flowering period followed by intermittent blooms until late summer.

- **Climbing and rambling roses**
  These have long, lax stems that need to be tied to their support structure. Ramblers flower once in early summer, with multiple small blooms in clusters. Climbers flower repeatedly throughout the summer, often with progressively larger and more fragrant blooms.

Perennials

Many perennials are also at their flowering peak in summer. The *Dianthus* family includes some highly fragrant flowering pinks, such as 'Mrs. Sinkins,' 'Doris,' and 'Gran's Favourite,' which smell predominantly of cloves. *Hemerocallis citrina* and *H.* 'Hyperion' both have sweetly scented, yellow flowers and long, architectural, straplike green leaves. Several fragrant varieties of *Hosta* bloom in summer, including *H.* 'Honeybells' and 'Royal Standard,' which both have a light, sweet scent. *Paeonia* 'Sarah Bernhardt,' with its beautiful large, double, rich pink flowers, is one of the few peonies with a heavy fragrance.

Perennial bulbs that flower fragrantly in summer include *Galtonia candicans* and lilies (*Lilium*), which come in all sizes and colors. Most are heavily fragrant and will fill the air with perfume on a warm day. They grow well in pots and can be moved into a prominent position near a doorway or seating area or plunged into the border while they are in full bloom and then retired to a corner to die down again. Make full use of plants such as these to fill in gaps in your patio display or to add color and interest to a dull spot in the garden.

Summer weather and its effects

The bonus of the summer is the warm sunshine, giving the perfect excuse to spend time outdoors, but the heat can be too intense at times, causing discomfort to anyone exposed to it and damage to plants that cannot escape it. There are many fragrant trees (in sizes to suit the garden) and climbing plants that can be trained over a frame or wires to give shade where it is needed. This might be over the seating area or in the part of the garden that receives the hottest midday sun. Dappled shade is preferable for the plants below, as a total exclusion of light is as bad as too much strong sunlight, so look for small-leaved plants that allow some light to pass through.

Jobs for summer

The long, warm days of summer are ideal for gardening, and an evening spent outside after a day at work—especially if you work indoors in an office—is a great way to unwind. The mad energy of spring has given way to steady growth, and the plants' main need now is for water. Other jobs include training and pruning plants so that you get the best possible growth and display of flowers. Because spending time in the garden during the warm summer months is such a pleasure, you may also enjoy taking on a larger project at this time, such as constructing a scented arch or fragrant seat. Another delightful summer job is harvesting, because this is the best time to select and dry fragrant leaves and foliage for use later in the year.

Watering

Plants rely on water to live, both because they need to drink their "food" in a solution of water through their roots and because they require moisture to keep their cell structure intact. Without sufficient water, the cells begin to lose their ability to support the plant, which we see as wilting. Regular wilting causes slow, stunted growth, poor flowers, and susceptibility to pest and disease attack. Plants in containers are even more vulnerable than those in the soil, because their roots are unable to seek out extra moisture in the surrounding area.

All plants need regular, reliable watering, especially during dry periods, although you can help reduce moisture loss by mulching the soil surface or planting ground cover. Watering plants in the evening is a relaxing activity, but you can automate the watering system if needed. Install a timer to switch on the water supply so that it is delivered to the plants in the late evening or early morning so the water has time to soak in before the soil heats up again. If you have containers, water can be delivered directly into the pots using narrow tubing so that none is spilled.

Training

New plants that were introduced in spring need to be tied to their supports as they grow. Climbers, in particular, need to be tied in to keep them from being damaged; frequent tying and regular training will help them look attractive and under control.

Pruning

Early summer is the ideal time to prune spring-flowering shrubs. Remove the shoots that have flowered as they die off. This allows the plant the maximum time to produce more shoots. Other flowering plants, such as annuals, should be deadheaded immediately after the first blooms have finished to encourage secondary flowers to develop quickly.

Providing shade

South-facing sunrooms can become very hot during the summer, so you may need to protect the plants inside by applying shading over the glass. You can use netting that unrolls outside, blinds on the inside, or thin white paint on the glass itself. South-facing windowsills in the house also become very hot, so plants should be chosen carefully for their ability to withstand the heat.

This Wisteria floribunda *should be pruned in the summer (and again in the winter) to help it develop flowering spurs for the following year.*

Low-growing thymes (Thymus) *can be planted in gaps among paving slabs. When stepped on, they will release a burst of fragrance.*

Harvesting

By midsummer, your efforts will be rewarded when your plants begin to thrive. If you are growing herbs and plants with fragrant foliage for drying, now is the time to begin harvesting nonflowering stems. Gather aromatic herbs such as mint and oregano in bunches of about ten stems, secure them with a rubber band, and hang them in a warm, airy spot to dry. The foliage can be used later in the year when fresh herbs are not available. Others, such as chive leaves and borage flowers, can be finely chopped and frozen into ice cubes for use in cooking or iced drinks. (See also Harvesting & Drying, pages 28–31.)

Construction

Fragrance can be incorporated into the garden in many ways, so take this into consideration if you are planning to build any structures or lay any paving during the summer. Pergolas, arches, and walkways are ideal for growing scented plants because they bring the fragrance up to eye level, making it stronger and easier to appreciate. Gaps can be left among new paving slabs or bricks so that low-growing plants with fragrant foliage or flowers can be introduced. This softens the harsh outline of the paving as well as giving scent, and many of the low-growing thymes will tolerate being stepped on periodically, releasing a burst of fragrant oil from their leaves.

Propagation & planting

Summer is a busy time for propagation, including sowing seeds, taking soft-tip and semiripe cuttings, layering, and dividing. By now, with the danger of frost having passed, any bedding plants and cuttings you were raising in the greenhouse or cold frame should have been moved outside. This will leave you space in the greenhouse to grow crops of tender plants such as tomatoes. The warm weather also means it is safe to plant out half-hardy annuals and autumn-flowering bulbs. In addition, many plants that need indoor protection during the colder months of the year will enjoy spending the summer outside, where they can bask in the sunshine and be washed clean by gentle summer rain.

Seedlings

Sow seeds of biennials, such as foxglove (*Digitalis*) and wallflower (*Erisymum*), to prepare them for being planted out in autumn. If large numbers of plants are required, sow the seeds outdoors in drills and thin them out after germination so that the plants are 4–6 in. apart when they are ready for transplanting. If only a few plants are needed, grow them in seed trays before transferring them to pots so that they can continue growing until they are ready to be transplanted.

Cuttings

Take cuttings while the shoots are growing rather than flowering. Once the hormone balance within the plant shifts from growing to flowering, the cuttings take longer to root, and cuttings of flowering shoots will seldom root at all.

Soft-tip cuttings

These are taken from the tips of the growing shoots. Strip the lower third of leaves and place the cutting in a tray or pot of compost. Take soft-tip cuttings of tender perennials so that they can be overwintered indoors or in a cool greenhouse.

Semiripe cuttings

These are taken from growing tip or side shoots where the wood has started to harden and turn brown. Aim for ½ in. of brown stem at the base of the cutting. Take semiripe cuttings of lavender (*Lavandula*), sage (*Salvia*), and *Helichrysum*.

Layering

Some fragrant plants that are difficult to root from cuttings, such as *Chimonanthus praecox* and *Hamamelis*, can be propagated by layering in late spring and early summer. Choose shoots that are at least one year old and bend them down so that a portion of the stem can be buried in the soil until it forms a new root system over a period of about twelve to eighteen months. When the new roots have formed, the layer can be severed from the parent plant and transplanted to grow independently.

To make this method of propagation work more effectively, the stem connecting the parent plant to the proposed new plant must be constricted in some way, in order to convince the plant that a section of stem will die if it does not produce roots. This can be

Sweet peas (Lathyrus odoratus) *can be grown outside greenhouses to provide fragrant shade from the summer sun.*

done by constricting the section of stem that is pulled down and covered by soil in one of three ways: by removing a narrow ring of bark, by circling the stem with tightly bound wire, or by splitting or twisting the stem. These are all methods of restricting the flow of food into the end of the layer, forcing it to root.

Division

Summer is the time to divide plants like the German iris (*Iris germanica* cultivars) immediately after the flowers have withered and died. Wash the roots gently and replant only the newest sections of rhizome, discarding all old or diseased sections of the plant and those pieces that have just flowered. Replant immediately and water well.

Planting out

Early summer, once the danger of late frost has finally passed, is the time to plant out half-hardy annuals that have been hardened off during the day but have been under cover at night. You should also plant autumn-flowering bulbs such as autumn crocus (*Colchicum autumnale*) into pots, borders, or in the lawn to naturalize. Most of these flower without leaves, so mark the planting spot with a stone or cane to prevent inadvertent damage.

Try to avoid planting large trees and shrubs during the driest months of summer because they may not establish due to lack of moisture around the roots. If you must plant trees and shrubs in summer, sink a piece of pipe vertically down next to the roots as you refill the hole with soil so that you can deliver water directly to where it is needed.

Greenhouses and sunrooms

You may wish to move some indoor plants outside to enjoy the warm summer weather. Although they still prefer a sunny corner because cold winds will damage them, *Citrus*, *Bougainvillaea*, oleander (*Nerium oleander*), and *Lantana* can all stand outside. This "rest" outside is also a good opportunity to use sprays on these plants to control pests or diseases.

Moving plants outside will also leave you space for crops of early tomatoes and tender plants such as peppers. You can shade the outside of the greenhouse naturally with sweet peas (*Lathyrus odoratus*), which will scramble up netting without blocking too much light inside. Known as friendship plants, sweet peas actually produce more flowers the more you cut them because they do not set seeds, so you can give bunches of these fragrant blooms away to family and friends.

Rose walkway

It can be a challenge to use every bit of available space in a garden, and a structure such as a rose walkway can really earn its keep by being both attractive and fragrant, as well as useful. It is an ideal way to link one area of the garden with another all year round, as well as provide shade and shelter during the summer months when the plants are in full growth.

WHAT YOU NEED
Tools: Spade, pruning shears
Materials: Metal arches or similar support structure, plants, slow-release fertilizer, string

As a feature, a rose walkway will become even more attractive as it ages, especially if you choose rose cultivars selected for both color and scent to adorn the sides and cover the top of the walkway. The scent is particularly important, because much of the fragrance will be released between 3–10 ft. above the ground into the area where it can be fully appreciated by most people. Climbing roses such as *Rosa* 'Zepherine Drouhin' and *R.* 'Albertine' are ideal.

Consideration must also be given to the growth rate and habit of the plants to give even and balanced growth along the walkway. It is particularly important that the climbing roses be tied to the structure, not intertwined through it, because this makes maintenance of the structure much easier. It will then be possible to treat the structure with a preservative or to carry out any repairs by removing the roses and repositioning them afterward. Plant maintenance, such as pruning and training, is also much easier if the roses are not intertwined through the structure.

Tip: If you need to remove the roses to carry out maintenance work on the support structure of the walkway, it is best to do so at the same time of year as the roses are pruned in order to minimize disturbance to the plants.

Erect the supporting structure according to the manufacturer's instructions. Here, metal arches are installed along a path. Dig a hole large enough to accommodate the plant's root system 12–16 in. away from the upright support.

Holding the plant by its woody stems, gently remove it from the container, teasing out any roots that are curling around the bottom of the rootball. Place the rootball in the hole and lean the top of the plant against the support.

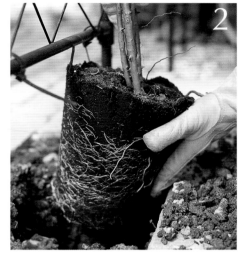

Using a spade, pull the soil back into the hole around the plant's rootball and pack it gently into place. Sprinkle a liberal dressing of slow-release fertilizer onto the soil. This will be washed down into the root zone as the plant's roots start to spread out.

Spread out the strongest leading shoots against the support frame. Tie them into position so that they will start climbing in the right direction.

Continue to tie in any main shoots, as well as side shoots to fill any gaps between the main shoots. This will give an even spread of growth over the whole support frame.

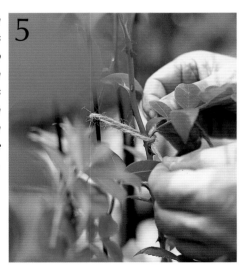

As they develop, tie in new growths and cut out any surplus or badly damaged shoots. Reduce any thin shoots to about one third of their original length. This will encourage them to produce more strong growth.

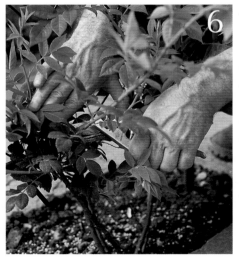

Flowering step lawn

Taking on a sloping garden can seem like a daunting task, but rather than viewing the slope as a problem, try to see the design possibilities it offers. Aim to work with the slope rather than against it by trying to level it out, which could well involve a great deal of time, effort, and expense. Creating a stepped lawn will transform the slope into an attractive and more functional feature and has the added advantage that fragrant plants can be incorporated into its design.

WHAT YOU NEED
Tools: String, wooden stakes, hammer, length of wood, level, spade
Materials: Stones, bricks, or similar material; fragrant plants such as *Dianthus* and *Thymus*

It is possible to cope with a sloping garden as long as a compromise can be reached over the work involved, such as having a lawn only where it is feasible to mow and trying to reduce the angle of the slope. Often by undertaking some minor adjustments to the levels, you can create a small terrace or series of terraces to make the slope into a feature. This could involve leveling some of the slope with soil held in place by a series of low retaining walls. The material used for these walls (such as stone or brick) can be chosen to blend in with the garden and its surroundings.

The height and distance between the steps will vary according to the angle of the slope. The steps will be much closer together on a steep slope and farther apart on a gentle slope. A stepped lawn can work perfectly on either a small or large scale, not only making maintenance easier but also providing the perfect setting for a range of low-growing fragrant plants without the need for separate borders.

> **Tip:** Use fragrant plants that prefer well-drained soil. *Dianthus*, for example, will thrive in planting pockets within a retaining wall because the wall provides good drainage.

Decide on the position of the steps according to the angle of the slope—a steep site will require more steps closer together. Mark out the "step lines" on the slope with string and stakes. The steps do not have to be placed at regular intervals if you want an informal design.

Check the levels to get some idea of how high the "riser" (the front of the step) will be. Ideally, it should be no more than 12 in. to make climbing easier. The size of the "tread" (the part of the step you walk on) can be any convenient distance.

Dig a trench along the step line wide enough for the stones to fit into. Peel back the turf on the upper side of the slope by 1–2 ft., depending on the angle of the slope.

Place the stones in position to form the riser of the step. Bed the stones into the bottom of the trench so that at least half of each stone is buried. Pack soil firmly into place around them.

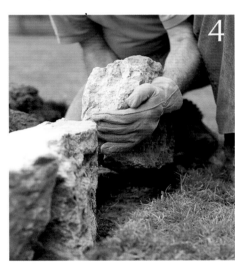

Add more soil to raise the level of the soil behind the riser to about 2 in. below the tops of the stones. Prepare the exposed soil behind the riser to a fine tilth and re-lay the turf, gently firming it into position.

Finish off the steps by planting a series of low-growing fragrant plants into the pockets between the stones.

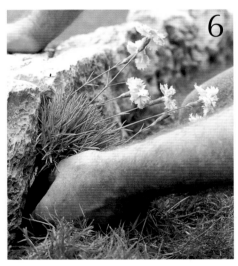

Container gardening

Patios, balconies, and roof gardens are all places where hard surfaces dominate, leaving less scope for plants. The patio usually consists of an area set aside in a sunny spot, either next to the house or in another part of the garden, to provide a stable base for furniture for sitting and/or eating. Balconies and roof gardens may have more variable weather conditions because their situation is determined by the building rather than the direction of the sun. Whatever the location, you can make these areas as fragrant as the traditional garden by choosing appropriate plants for the wide range of attractive containers available.

Balconies and roof gardens

The main considerations for a balcony or roof garden are weight and stability, which may restrict the size of container, particularly if the site is exposed to regular strong wind. Precautions you can take include using containers with a wide, stable base, staking taller plants firmly when you plant them, and keeping tall plants away from the edge. Another good idea is to fix trellises to the side walls to reduce the wind flow, with plastic mesh on the outside if necessary (it can be hidden behind plants on the inside).

Types of containers

There is a vast choice of containers available to suit everyone's taste. Terra cotta looks attractive and comes in natural, earthy colors, but make sure it is frostproof or it may crack during the winter. Being porous, it allows the compost to lose moisture through the sides of the pot as well as from the surface, which can mean extra watering. Glazed pottery pots come in many colors and are ideal if you are designing around a color theme and using matching paint on a trellis or other woodwork.

Plastic pots are lightweight, come in various colors, and keep the compost moist because water is not lost through the sides. They may not look as natural as pottery containers, but they can be painted or disguised beneath the foliage. They will last many years, although they may become brittle if they are in direct sunlight. Metal containers vary in weight and hold moisture well. However, they also conduct heat well, and if they are in direct sunlight, the roots inside can get very hot, resulting in damage.

Fragrant container plants

Most plants can be grown successfully in a container as long as they are looked after properly. Some of the best fragrant plants for growing in containers are:

*   **Indoor fragrant plants**
    Freesia, Lilium, Hoya, Gardenia, Hyacinthus, Stephanotis, Citrus limon, Narcissus, Iris reticulata, and *Jasminum.*

*   **Outdoor fragrant plants**
    Abeliophyllum, Hamamelis, Laurus nobilis, Myrtus, Narcissus, Nicotiana, Sarcococca, Daphne, Lavandula, and *Artemisia.*

This cast-metal container has an intricate pattern of twining leaves that adds an extra decorative touch to a patio garden.

You do not have to restrict yourself to small plants in a container garden. Many smaller tree varieties will thrive in a container if well cared for.

Compost

The type of compost you use in your containers is more of a consideration on a balcony or roof garden than on a patio where weight does not matter.

Loamless composts

These are based on peat or coir rather than soil. Their advantages are that they weigh much less than loam-based compost and give good root aeration. However, they dry out quickly in hot weather, can be difficult to keep moist, and do not hold on to nutrients. They can also be unstable, especially when dry. Plants growing in this type of compost need more frequent watering and feeding.

Loam-based composts

These are heavy and therefore more stable than loamless composts. They also retain moisture and nutrients well. Loam-based composts are available in different strengths, so you can suit the compost to the plant being grown, from annual bedding to long-term fruit trees.

Growing plants in paving

You do not need a large garden to grow aromatic and fragrant plants. In fact, it is not necessary to have a garden at all, as many smaller plants can be grown in the cracks and crevices of walls or paving. These low-growing, ground-cover plants are ideal for softening the harsh outlines of an area of hard landscaping, such as a path or patio, which can look bare, especially when it is first laid.

WHAT YOU NEED
Tools: Small chisel, pointing trowel, brush, watering can or hose
Materials: Plants such as *Dianthus*, *Phlox*, *Viola odorata*, *Thymus*, and *Chamaemelum*; compost

If you are laying a new path or patio, you can leave gaps in the paving where plants can be positioned. In areas already surfaced, you will need to chip out some sand and mortar from the joints of the paving in order to create pockets for planting. How much sand and mortar is taken out will depend on the technique that was used to lay the paving and the type of base beneath, which must be broken through to allow adequate drainage for the plants. Soil may need to be dug out of the joint as well, but again, this depends on the method used when the paving was laid.

Encouraging plants to establish in pockets and allowing them to spread is also an attractive way of controlling weeds. The spreading plants will colonize the joints, depriving weed seeds of room to germinate and grow. Roman chamomile (*Chamaemelum nobile*) and garden thyme (*Thymus vulgaris*) will grow and spread quickly and are resilient enough to tolerate being walked on occasionally. Plants such as *Lavandula* x *intermedia* will provide fragrance and aroma, while *Oenothera triloba* produces a strong violet scent in the evening.

> **Tip:** Do not be tempted to use invasive plants, such as larger members of the mint family (*Mentha*), because they may undermine the paved area.

Using a small chisel, carefully chip out the mortar from the joint in the paving where the plant is to be positioned, taking great care to minimize disturbance to the surrounding hard surface.

With a pointing trowel, scrape out the sand and mortar from the opened joint in the paving. It is important to remove as much rubble as possible to create a pocket for the plant's roots to grow in.

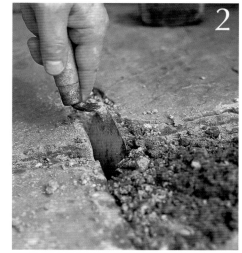

Knock the plant from its pot and remove as much soil as possible, gently teasing out the roots. This makes the rootball as small as possible so that it can be lowered down into the planting pocket in the paving.

Using your fingers, gently insert the plant into the pocket. Press it into position and firm it into place. Let the plant sit slightly higher than the surface of the paving to allow for settling.

Use a brush to fill the rest of the planting pocket with compost. Tug the top of the plant gently a few times to coax more compost down around the roots of the plant.

Water the plant to help settle the compost around the roots. If all the compost washes down into the planting pocket, you may need to add more to the hole and water it in.

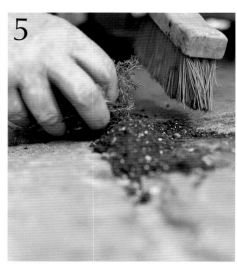

Citrus specimen plant

Citrus plants are ideal for growing in the house or sunroom. Species such as *Citrus limon* have wonderful glossy leaves and attractive flowers that are pink in bud, opening to pure white. The flowers are also highly fragrant and release a jonquil scent, so they are an excellent choice for filling a room with natural fragrance.

WHAT YOU NEED
Tools: Pruning shears, water sprayer, soft cloth or tissue
Materials: Citrus plant, garden cane, string, washing detergent, leaf-shine solution, fertilizer

In mild climates, citrus plants can be given the protection of an indoor environment through the winter and then moved outdoors from late spring until early fall. As with other plants, much of their growth is regulated by light level and temperature, but most citrus plants slip into dormancy when temperatures fall below 55°F. Species such as the *Citrus limon* used in this project will produce as many as five flushes of flowers each year, so it is not uncommon to see flower buds, flowers, and fruit on the same plant at any given time.

Although citrus plants are both attractive and have very fragrant flowers, they do require care and attention to keep them growing well. The fact that they are constantly growing and have a natural tendency to form an open, straggly habit means that they need regular pruning and training if they are to form a strong branch structure that can cope with the weight of the fruits when they are produced.

Tip: Great care must be taken if citrus trees are to be severely pruned, because they have very limited food reserves in their woody tissue and removing a number of branches may lead to severe dieback of some of the remaining branches.

With new or young plants, start by tying the main central stem to a cane. Training the plant in this way helps to produce an upright stem on which a framework of branches can develop.

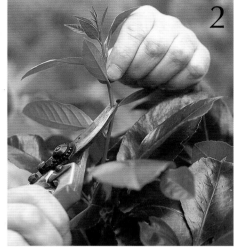

Snip off any shoots that may start to compete with the main stem and reduce side shoots by about one third of their length to encourage them to become thicker and more sturdy.

It is important to do as much pruning as necessary while the shoots are young and soft. Older branches may die back after pruning and be prone to attack by fungal disease. These branches will need to be pruned a second time to remove the dead growth.

Where leaves have accumulated a layer of dirt, spray with lukewarm water containing a weak solution of detergent to soften the dirt. Several applications may be needed.

Wipe the leaves with a soft cloth or tissue to clean the remaining dirt off the leaf surface. At this stage, a "leaf-shine" solution can be applied to improve the leaf gloss, if desired.

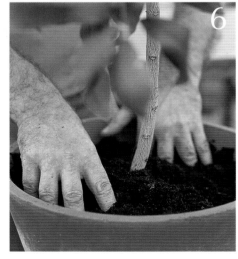

The plant will need a regular application of fertilizer and repotting because it is continuously growing, but only transfer it to a pot 1 in. larger in diameter than the existing one. A move to a much larger pot would result in lots of stem growth and fewer flowers.

Planting a fragrant container

Growing fragrant plants in containers offers the opportunity to bring scent to even the smallest garden; to bring fragrance close to the house, seating areas, and patios; and to cultivate the plants you want regardless of the soil in the rest of the garden. Some fragrant plants, such as sweet peas, roses, and jasmines, can also be grown "vertically," allowing you to overcome space limitations by using features such as trellises, tripods, and wigwams, which support the plants without taking up much room in the garden.

WHAT YOU NEED
Materials: Large container, multipurpose compost, sweet peas (*Lathyrus odoratus*), wigwam

Vertical gardening (growing upward rather than sideways) using supports allows plants to develop fully without taking up much room either in the garden or in a container on the patio. Ideally, the structure should be chosen to suit the plant it will support. This is especially important for plants with twining stems or tendrils, as there is a limit to the diameter of the support around which a plant can twine and grip—usually about the thickness of a pencil. Slender supports, such as thin wooden strips or bamboo canes, are ideal for plants such as sweet peas. They are strong enough to support the plants but thin enough to be obscured by foliage and flowers as the plants establish and cover the support.

A trellis wigwam covered in sweet peas makes a beautiful summer feature. Planting the peas inside the wigwam will cut down on maintenance time, as you will not need to tie the plants into position or provide extra support. This is because the plants will naturally grow out into the light, growing past the support structure and gripping onto it as they grow. The climbers will also become self-supporting, clinging to each other as well as onto the structure where the supports are too thick.

> **Tip:** In the fall, replant these containers with fragrant bulbs, such as *Narcissus* 'Pheasant's Eye,' to provide an excellent display of scent and color the following spring.

Start by selecting a suitable container and filling it with compost to within 4 in. of the rim (this should be the level after the compost has been gently packed).

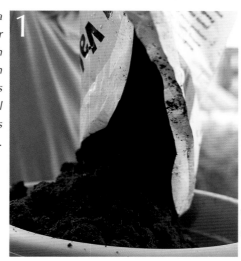

When the compost is up to the required level, remove the sweet peas from their pots and place them in the container, about 3–4 in. inside the rim. Plant them into the compost and then firm them into position.

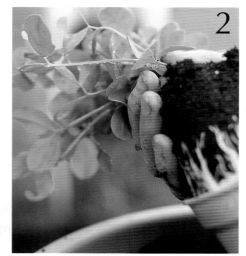

Position the base frame for the wigwam onto the rim of the pot and assemble it using small nuts and bolts. Leave the joints loose to allow for some adjustment when the wigwam is erected over the container.

Place the wigwam struts into their slots in the base frame and push them about 3 in. into the compost to give the wigwam greater stability.

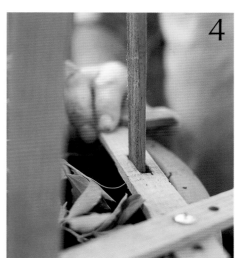

When all of the upright struts of the wigwam have been assembled and slotted into the base frame, gather them together at the top around a central finial and place a ring over the wigwam struts to hold them in position.

Planting the sweet peas inside the wigwam forces them to grow upward and outward, which means that their tendrils will cling to the wigwam as they grow through it.

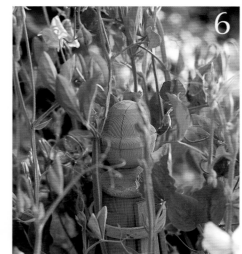

Herbs for health

Throughout history, herbs have been used for medicinal purposes and to promote a feeling of well-being. Early monasteries and apothecary shops depended on having herb gardens to make potions. Some of the medicines in common use today have been synthesized from chemicals found in plants. If you enjoy cooking, you will also know that nothing beats the flavor of homegrown herbs. Keeping a variety of different herbs in pots or a bed close to the kitchen or grill will allow you to pick them when they are needed to use fresh or to dry for later use.

Growing herbs

The herbs we grow at home originate from all over the world, so their growing requirements differ; most, however, prefer a sunny spot with well-drained soil and shelter from cold winds. Some, such as sweet basil (*Ocimum basilicum*), are only hardy in warm climates and need winter protection in colder areas. Others, like rosemary (*Rosmarinus officinalis*), are hardy in many regions, although they can still be affected by a cold snap.

Harvesting herbs

Once the plants are growing well, you can harvest them for drying as well as using them fresh. Some plants, like mint (*Mentha*), are so quick-growing that you may even find you are drying enough to supply friends and family as well as your own cupboard. All you need is a warm, dark place to hang the stems as they dry and some airtight jars in which to store the crumbled leaves once they are ready (see pages 28–31 for more information on harvesting and drying).

Herbal teas

Many herbs can be used dried or fresh to make refreshing drinks that can be drunk hot or iced for pleasure or medicinal purposes. Roman chamomile (*Chamaemelum nobile*) is one of the most popular because it calms an upset stomach and anxious nerves, as well as aiding a good night's sleep. Teas made from sage (*Salvia officinalis*) help concentration and are a good gargle for a sore throat. To make a single serving of chamomile or sage tea, add 1 tsp. of the herb leaves to 1 cup of water. Boil the water, wait thirty seconds, then sprinkle the leaves onto the water to steep, stirring periodically, for ten minutes. Use a china or glass cup and pure water for the best results. Strain and drink it without milk, but sweeten with honey if you like.

Herb pillows

These date back to the days when sweet-smelling herbs were added to straw pillows in order to repel insects. Today, a small pillow or sachet is ideal for hanging near the bed at night to relax you. You can make a pillow to suit your individual needs, using a combination of leaves and flowers such as English lavender (*Lavandula angustifolia*), garden mignonette (*Reseda odorata*), rosemary (*Rosmarinus officinalis*), and lemon verbena (*Aloysia triphylla*).

Jasmine flowers have an exquisite fragrance that can lift the spirits. This Jasminum x stephanense *is a hardy variety with pinkish flowers.*

Herbal baths

An aromatic herbal bath can be both pleasurable and therapeutic, especially after a busy day in the garden. Tie a large handful of leaves in a square of muslin cloth and hang it under the running water as the bath fills. To relax, try Roman chamomile (*Chamaemelum nobile*), jasmine (*Jasminum officinale*), lime flowers (*Tilia*), or valerian (*Valeriana*). For stimulation, use sweet basil (*Ocimum basilicum*), bay (*Laurus nobilis*), fennel (*Foeniculum vulgare*), lavender (*Lavandula angustifolia*), lemon balm (*Melissa officinalis*), lemon verbena (*Aloysia triphylla*), mint (*Mentha*), rosemary (*Rosmarinus officinalis*), sage (*Salvia officinalis*), or thyme (*Thymus vulgaris*). Healing herbs include pot marigold (*Calendula officinalis*), spearmint (*Mentha spicata*), and yarrow (*Achillea millefolium*).

The fruit-scented, creamy yellow flowers of the lime tree (Tilia) *are perfect ingredients for a relaxing herbal bath.*

Herbal medicine

Many over-the-counter medicines are based on herbs. For example, in the past people used to chew a piece of willow bark to cure headaches. Investigation disclosed the presence of salicylic acid, which is now used to manufacture aspirin. Other herbal remedies include calendula ointment for cuts and grazes, arnica ointment for bruises and sprains, and aloe vera gel for sunburn. Fresh from the garden, you can use plantain leaves (*Plantago*) on insect bites, feverfew leaves (*Tanacetum parthenium*) for migraine, and mint (*Mentha*) for indigestion.

Companion planting

When plants are grown for their fragrance, the last thing you need is for the natural scent to be masked or impeded, which can happen when plants are sprayed with pesticides to control insect attacks. One solution to this problem is to grow plants together as companions in order to reduce or even eliminate the need to spray. Scented plants are frequently used as companion plants to attract pests away from vegetables.

WHAT YOU NEED
Tools: Trowel, bulb planter, or spade
Materials: Plants (see box below)

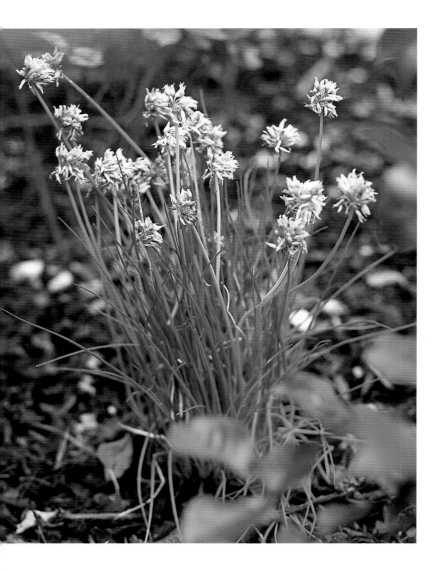

The chemical taint of pesticides can linger for days after spraying. It will have its own (usually unpleasant) smell and will certainly deter anyone from sampling the fragrance of even the most scented flowers. To make matters worse, some of these pesticides will kill or deter beneficial pollinating insects as well as the pest that has been targeted. Companion planting—where plants are grown together to protect one another from infestation by pests or attack by diseases—is therefore a good solution. Companion plants work in two different ways: as host plants or as repellent plants. Host plants are attractive to certain pests and diseases and, because of that attraction, draw them away from the plants that require protection. Repellent plants work by driving pests and diseases away from certain areas or plants. In both cases, it is often the aroma or fragrance of these companion plants that has the desired effect.

Cultivated plants	Companion plants
Apple	Wallflower
Broad bean	Carrot, Celery
Cabbage	Beet, Chard
Lettuce	Carrot, Radish
Potato	Nasturtium, Tagetes
Raspberry	Marigold
Rose	Calendula, Chives, Garlic, Tagetes
Strawberry	Borage, Onion
Sunflower	Cucumber, Corn
Tomato	Basil, Carrot

Dig a hole large enough to accommodate the companion plant's root system. For smaller plants, a trowel or a bulb planter will be perfect for this. For larger plants, use a spade.

If the pot containing the companion plant is overcrowded, you can divide it into several clumps that can then be planted throughout the bed of cultivated plants. In this example, chives are being planted in a bed of roses.

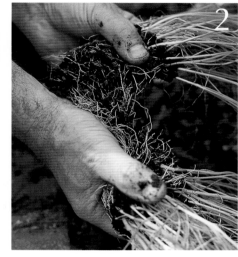

Holding the plant by its rootball, place it in the hole with the base of the rootball on the floor of the hole.

Pull the soil back into the hole around the plant and pack gently into place. Make sure that the surface of the rootball is covered by soil. Water the plant to help settle the soil around the roots.

Wallflowers are often planted alongside members of the apple family to encourage pollinating insects. The insects are attracted to the early flowering wallflowers and then transfer to the apples when they come into bloom.

Nasturtiums are often planted among potatoes to attract the aphid population to them and away from the potatoes. The nasturtiums are, in effect, used as "sacrifice" plants to protect the potatoes, but their fragrance is a welcome bonus.

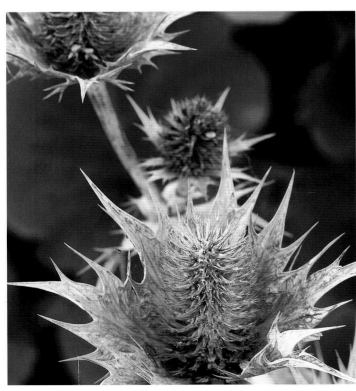

TREES

KEY INFORMATION

H: The average height the plant can reach

S: The average spread the plant can achieve

Sun/partial shade/shade: The position the plant prefers

Well-drained/moderate/moist/ water (for aquatics): How much water the plant needs

Acid/alkaline/neutral/any: The plant's preferred soil type

Z1 to Z10: The minimum winter temperature (zone) the plant can withstand

Zone 1: below –50°F
Zone 2: –50 to –40°F
Zone 3: –40 to –30°F
Zone 4: –30 to –20°F
Zone 5: –20 to –10°F
Zone 6: –10 to 0°F
Zone 7: 0 to 10°F
Zone 8: 10 to 20°F
Zone 9: 20 to 30°F
Zone 10: 30 to 40°F

Drimys winteri
H 46 ft. S 32 ft.
Sun/partial shade
Well-drained
Any Z8

A native of South America, this relative of the magnolia is a vigorous tree with an upright habit and strongly aromatic ash-gray bark. The tough, leathery evergreen leaves are broadly lance-shaped, up to 8 in. long, a dull dark green above and bluish-white beneath. From late spring into summer, creamy white flowers with a jasmine-like fragrance are produced in clusters of up to twenty blooms on the tips of shoots. Propagate by sowing seeds in a cold frame in autumn or taking semiripe tip cuttings in summer.

Hoheria glabrata
H 23 ft. S 23 ft.
Sun/partial shade
Well-drained/moderate
Alkaline/neutral Z8

This is a magnificent small tree from the south island of New Zealand. Its lax, flexible branches give it a broad, spreading, graceful habit. The deciduous glossy, dark green leaves are up to 4 in. long, broadly oval in shape, but tapering to a point at the tip. In early to midsummer, large numbers of fragrant, translucent white flowers up to 2 in. across are produced in such profusion that they weigh down the branches. Propagate by sowing seeds into pots and placing them in a cold frame in autumn or by taking semiripe cuttings in late summer or early autumn.

Magnolia* x *veitchii
H 82 ft. S 46 ft.
Sun/partial shade
Moderate
Acid/neutral Z6

This cultivated hybrid has some
characteristics of both its parents,
M. campbellii and *M. denudata*.
It has an erect habit when young,
changing to an open, spreading
habit with age. The large,
deciduous, spear-shaped leaves are
tinted with purple when young,
changing to mid-green with a paler
coating on the underside as they
mature. In early summer, it
produces large, erect, goblet-shaped
white flowers flushed with pink
markings that are very sweetly
scented. *M.* x *veitchii* 'Isca' has
white flowers with pink markings
at the base of each petal. Propagate
by taking semiripe cuttings in late
summer or by layering in spring.

***Robinia pseudoacacia* 'Frisia'**
H 32 ft. S 16 ft.
Sun
Moderate
Any Z5

The black locust or false acacia
is a quick-growing tree that can
sucker freely. Its young shoots have
wine-red spines, and the bark of the
trunk becomes deeply furrowed as
the plant ages. The pinnate leaves
change from golden yellow as they
emerge to greenish-yellow in
summer, then orange-yellow in
autumn. Fragrant, white, pealike
flowers are produced in long,
hanging clusters in summer,
followed by brown seed pods. It
can be pruned hard in early spring
each year to control the size and
produce larger leaves, or in summer
(to avoid excessive bleeding) to
maintain health. Propagate by
grafting in winter.

Tilia* x *euchlora
H 65 ft. S 46 ft.
Sun/partial shade
Moderate
Alkaline/neutral Z4

This hybrid lime makes an elegant
tree when young, then develops a
rounded, dense, straggly habit with
low, hanging branches drooping
almost to ground level as it ages.
The broadly oval-shaped leaves
have a finely toothed margin and
are glossy, dark green on the upper
surface and pale green on the
underside. The sweetly scented,
yellowish-white flowers are
produced in small clusters in
midsummer. This lime remains
free of aphids, so there is no sticky
"honeydew," and the flowers often
make honeybees drowsy. Propagate
by budding and grafting or by
layering in spring.

SHRUBS

Cytisus battandieri
H 10 ft. S 7 ft.
Sun
Moderate
Any Z7

The pineapple broom is a small tree or large shrub grown for its pealike, golden yellow, pineapple-scented flowers that are carried in tight clusters on the tips of branches. The deciduous leaves are three-lobed and covered with a layer of fine silky hairs when young, giving them an attractive silver sheen that changes to a dull green as they age. The dull-green stems have a stiff, erect habit and often turn a corky brown as they age. Prune after flowering, although note that this plant does not recover from hard pruning into older wood. Propagate by taking semiripe cuttings in summer.

Genista aetnensis
H 26 ft. S 26 ft.
Sun
Well-drained/moderate
Any Z8

The Mt. Etna broom is a large, elegant, rounded, deciduous shrub with an upright habit and slender, drooping, bright green branches that are practically leafless. The tough, sparse leaves are mid-green in color and straplike, with fine, white, silky hairs produced only on the youngest shoots. Heavily scented, pealike flowers are a golden yellow color and produced in large quantities on the tips of shoots in mid- and late summer. If pruning this plant, do not cut into old wood, because it will not regrow. Propagate by sowing seeds in spring.

Lavandula angustifolia
H 3 ft. S 3 ft.
Sun
Well-drained/moderate
Alkaline/neutral Z5

The English lavender has long, narrow, aromatic, silver-gray leaves covered with fine, feltlike hairs that are very effective for preventing moisture loss. The small, tubelike flowers are carried in narrow clusters (spikes) on tough square stems. The form _L. a._ 'Hidcote' has strongly scented, deep purple-blue flowers and a compact, bushy habit. There is a white-flowered form, _L. a._ 'Alba,' and the pink _L. a._ 'Rosea.' Propagate by taking semiripe heel cuttings in late summer.

Philadelphus coronarius
H 10 ft. S 8 ft.
Sun/partial shade
Moderate
Any Z5

The sweet mock orange is a deciduous bushy shrub with a dense, upright habit and thin, twiggy stems that carry mid-green, oval leaves. In summer, the dense spikes of small, creamy white flowers are noted for their sweet, heady fragrance. There are a number of cultivars with attractively colored leaves, including *P. c.* 'Aureus,' with pale, golden yellow leaves that turn lemon green as they age, and *P. c.* 'Variegatus,' which has mid-green leaves decorated with an attractive broad white margin. Propagate by taking semiripe cuttings in summer or hardwood cuttings in autumn.

Rosa rugosa
H 8 ft. S 13 ft.
Sun/partial shade
Moderate
Any Z2

The rugosa rose is a very tough, dense, vigorous rose with a spreading, suckering habit. The light, gray-brown shoots are densely covered with fine bristly thorns (it is also commonly called the hedgehog rose) that carry leathery, deeply veined, glossy dark green leaves that turn orange in autumn. The large, single, deep pink flowers have an open cup shape with a bright golden yellow center, and are followed in the fall by large, round, bright red hips. The cultivar 'Hansa' has very fragrant semidouble scarlet flowers. Propagate by taking semiripe cuttings in summer or hardwood cuttings in winter or spring.

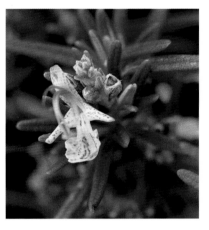

Rosmarinus officinalis
H 5 ft. S 5 ft.
Sun
Well-drained/moderate
Any Z6

This is the popular cottage garden rosemary that grows with a strong spreading habit, developing into an open-centered shrub with age. The blue-green evergreen foliage is strongly aromatic and very useful in both cooking and herbal treatments. Each leaf is narrow and leathery, a suitable adaptation to resist moisture loss in the hot Mediterranean regions from which the species originates. In late spring and early summer, small, two-lipped, pale lilac flowers are produced along the stems, sometimes with a second flush in autumn. Prune annually after the first flowering, especially if the foliage is to be harvested. Propagate by taking semiripe cuttings in summer.

CLIMBERS & WALL SHRUBS

Jasminum x _stephanense_
H 16 ft. S 10 ft.
Sun/partial shade
Well-drained
Any Z7

Found growing wild in southwest
China, this hybrid of _J. beesianum_
and _J. officinale_ is a vigorous woody
deciduous climber with a twining
habit. The leaves are arranged in
opposite pairs on green climbing
stems. They are dull green in color,
broadly lance-shaped, up to 2 in.
long, and arranged in groups of five
along a central rib. The clusters of
heavily fragrant, pale pink flowers
open to produce star-shaped blooms
1 in. across. Prune after flowering
by thinning out some of the older
shoots. Propagate by taking semiripe
cuttings in summer.

Lathyrus odoratus
H 7 ft. S 3 ft.
Sun
Well-drained
Any Z6

Originating from Italy, the annual
sweet pea is a tall, vigorous, self-
supporting climber with curling
tendrils on the tip of each mid-green
leaflet, with one pair of leaves.
The flowers are heavily scented
(especially in the evening) and
come in a variety of colors, with
pink, white, and deep purple
being the most popular. They are
produced in clusters throughout
the summer months. For vibrant
colors and the most scented flowers,
choose old-fashioned cultivars such
as 'Cupani' and 'Painted Lady.'
Propagate by sowing seeds in
autumn or spring and harden off
before planting out in late spring
or early summer.

Lonicera periclymenum
H 16 ft. S 16 ft.
Sun/partial shade
Moderate
Any Z4

The European honeysuckle is a
strong-growing, twining, woody
climber, ideal for a wall, fence,
or pergola, with oval, mid-green
deciduous leaves and heavily
fragrant, tubular flowers. These are
red and yellow-white, carried in
clusters at the ends of the shoots,
and followed by poisonous red
berries in autumn. In late spring
to early summer, the form _L. p._
'Belgica' has white flowers, flushed
red-purple outside and fading to
yellow, with a second display in
late summer. _L. p._ 'Serotina' flowers
midsummer to midautumn; the
flowers are rich red-purple outside
and white inside, fading to yellow.
Prune to maintain its shape by
removing old wood after flowering.
Propagate by taking hardwood
cuttings in autumn.

Rosa 'Albertine'
H 16 ft. S 13 ft.
Sun
Moderate
Acid Z7

Raised in France in 1921, this strong-growing deciduous rambling rose is one of the most reliable ever produced. It is ideal against a wall, trellis, or fence. The young growths produce copper-brown leaves on arching, red-thorned, dull-red shoots. The leaves turn a glossy mid-green later. The richly fragrant, salmon-pink flowers, which become paler with age, are fully double and about 3 in. across. Pruning involves cutting out the old flowered shoots immediately after flowering and removing any suckers that may originate from the rootstock of a grafted plant. These need to be removed at their base, or they will dominate the top variety. Propagate by taking hardwood cuttings in late autumn.

Trachelospermum jasminoides
H 26 ft. S 26 ft.
Sun
Moderate
Any Z8

The confederate jasmine is a handsome climbing plant with tough evergreen leaves that are a glossy dark green color and arranged in opposite pairs along thin, brown, twining stems. The small jasminelike flowers are very fragrant, white with a yellow eye in the center, and star-shaped. They are borne in profusion during early and midsummer. The cultivar *T. j.* 'Variegatum' has a narrow white margin at the edge of each leaf and also produces fragrant flowers. Propagate by taking softwood cuttings in summer or by layering young shoots in autumn.

Wisteria floribunda
H 32 ft. S 32 ft.
Sun/partial shade
Moderate
Alkaline/neutral Z5

This is one of the most beautiful of all climbing plants, particularly when draped in cascades of fragrant, pealike flowers in early summer as the leaves emerge. The leaves are dark to mid-green in color and divided into small leaflets. The plant grows best against a sunny wall. It supports itself with vigorous stems that twine in a clockwise direction and grow up to 32 ft. in length. The vanilla-scented flowers are white, reddish-pink, blue, or mauve. They open from the base toward the tip and fragrance can vary greatly between cultivars. *W. f.* 'Multijuga' is very fragrant. Propagate by layering, grafting, or taking softwood cuttings in summer.

PERENNIALS & BULBS

Achillea millefolium
H 2 ft. S 2 ft.
Sun
Moderate
Any Z2

Commonly known as yarrow, this
herbaceous perennial is an invasive,
mat-forming plant with lance-
shaped, finely divided, slightly hairy
leaves of a dull mid-green color.
The finely cut foliage has a pungent
aroma (feverfew) and is excellent for
use in potpourris. The musk-scented
flowers are held erect above the
foliage in bold, flat clusters 3–4 in.
across from early until late summer,
with colors ranging from deep reds
through lilacs to pinks. One very
popular form is _A. m._ 'Fanal,' which
has deep-red flowers, fading to
orange as they age. Propagate by
dividing in spring.

Artemisia 'Powis Castle'
H 2 ft. S 3 ft.
Sun
Well-drained/moderate
Any Z8

This pretty, woody-based perennial
has highly aromatic silver foliage
and is ideal for growing in a sunny
border. The leaves are very finely
divided, almost linear, and form a
fluffy, rounded mound that ruffles
with the slightest breeze and
releases its fragrant oils if the
foliage is touched. Small, silvery,
yellow-tinted flowers are produced
in clusters of up to 6 in. long
throughout late summer and fall.
This plant may be hard-pruned in
spring to keep it compact. Propagate
by taking soft-tip or heel cuttings in
summer, especially in frost-prone
areas where the plant may not
survive the winter.

Dianthus chinensis
H 18 in. S 12 in.
Sun
Well-drained/moderate
Alkaline/neutral Z4

These plants form tufted mounds of
silver-gray foliage, with thin leaves
arranged in pairs on slender, silver-
gray stems that are very narrow and
spiky. They are ideal for the front
of a border or bed because they
produce flushes of delicately
scented, brightly colored blooms
on thin stems up to 18 in. long, in
colors ranging from white through
many shades of pink to dark reds in
summer and again in fall. The
cultivar 'Doris' has double blooms
that are two-tone pink and heavily
scented of cloves. Propagate by
sowing seeds in spring or taking
cuttings of nonflowering shoots
in summer.

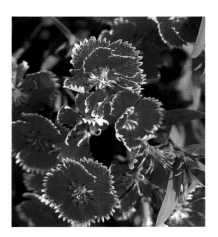

Dianthus gratianopolitanus
H 8 in. S 16 in.
Sun
Moderate
Alkaline/neutral Z5

This pretty, low-growing perennial
is known as the cheddar pink and
grows to form a dense, spreading
mat of small, narrow, spiky-looking
gray-green leaves on woody-based
stems. From late spring into summer,
solitary flowers are produced on
short, wiry stems, just above the
height of the leaves. They are
strongly scented of cloves, with a
toothed edge to each petal, and
come in shades of pink, often with
a darker ring of color in the center.
Propagate by sowing seeds or by
dividing in spring.

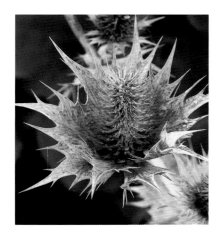

Eryngium maritimum
H 16–36 in. S 4 ft.
Sun
Well-drained
Any Z5

This clump-forming herbaceous
perennial has tough, prickly leaves
that vary in color from silver-gray
to gray-green, with the stems
showing the same variations in
color. In late summer, tufted globes
of metallic silver-blue flowers, each
surrounded by a ruff of leathery
spines, are produced on the shoot
tips, the dead flowers often lasting
well into the winter. These plants
are unusual in that they have
aromatic roots, producing a strong
scent of parsnips when exposed.
Propagate by taking root cuttings
or dividing in spring. Some species
are cultivated by seed.

Hedychium coronarium
H 10 ft. S 3 ft.
Sun/partial shade
Moderate/moist
Any Z9

The white gingerlily is an
herbaceous perennial that originates
from India. It has a thick, fleshy
rootstock and a narrow, upright
habit, with long, pointed, lance-
shaped, glossy green leaves that
often reach 18 in. in length. During
late summer, very fragrant, butterfly-
shaped flowers are produced on
spikes up to 8 in. long on stems
often 7 ft. tall. The flowers are white
with yellow markings at the base of
each petal. Propagate by sowing
seeds into pots as soon as it is ripe
and placing the pots in a cold
frame, or by dividing the rhizomes
in spring.

PERENNIALS & BULBS

Hemerocallis
H 3 ft. S 3 ft.
Sun/partial shade
Moderate
Any Z4

This colorful, clump-forming plant
has architectural, semievergreen,
pale to mid-green, strap-shaped
leaves ending in a sharp point
at the tip. The brightly colored
blooms only last for a single day
in midsummer but are produced
in such rapid succession that this is
hardly noticed. The lilylike flowers
are produced in clusters on top
of tall, erect stems. The species
H. lilioasphodelus and its hybrids
are particularly fragrant, with a
scent similar to honeysuckle.
H. citrina has very fragrant flowers
that open in late afternoon and
evening. Propagate by dividing
in autumn.

Hosta
H 3 ft. S 2 ft.
Partial shade
Moderate
Any Z6

This is one of the most beautiful
herbaceous perennials, with small,
trumpetlike, pendulous flowers
carried on tall green stems above
the leaves from midsummer.
These plants are grown for their
attractive foliage, and leaf shapes
range from long and narrow to oval
with a pointed tip. Colors vary from
blue to rich combinations of silver
or golden variegations. The form
'Honeybells' has fragrant white
flowers, sometimes striped blue,
and 'Invincible' has fragrant pale
mauve flowers. Propagate by
dividing in early spring.

Lilium
H 4 ft. S 10 in.
Sun/partial shade
Moderate
Any Z6

These glorious plants have bold,
trumpetlike blooms made up of
six petals that curl open to develop
into an open star shape that can
vary in size from 1–10 in. across,
depending on the variety. They are
among the most highly scented
flowers available. The leaves are
pale to dark green; some are
narrow, almost grasslike, and
grouped at the base of the plant,
while others produce leaves in
clusters (whorls) at intervals along
the stems that often reach 3 ft. tall,
topped by flowers in late summer
or early autumn. Propagate from
scales in autumn.

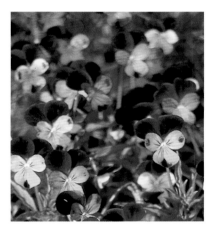

Salvia
H 12–60 in. S 9–24 in.
Sun
Well-drained/moderate
Any Z9

Salvia is a large genus of annuals, biennials, perennials, and shrubs, distinguished by their colorful two-lipped flowers in summer. Many have aromatic foliage, including *S. officinalis* (sage), which is used in cooking. The annual *S. viridis* 'Claryssa' is dwarf and bushy, with brightly colored bracts of purple, pink, or white. Bedding forms include *S. splendens* 'Blaze of Fire' and 'Red Arrows,' both with bright red flowers. Blue-flowered forms include *S. patens*, a tuberous perennial with hairy leaves, and *S. guaranitica*, a subshrub with long, deep blue flowers. Propagate annuals and perennials by sowing seeds in spring, and in summer for biennials. Take semiripe cuttings of shrubs in late summer.

Thymus
H 12 in. S 12 in.
Sun
Well-drained/moderate
Any Z5

This genus includes around 350 species of low-growing, hardy, evergreen herbaceous perennials and subshrubs with aromatic leaves. Some are mat-forming and prostrate; others form small shrubs with thin, twiggy stems. The small leaves are usually oval and gray-green, sometimes hairy. Mat-forming types form dense carpets. *Thymus* x *citriodorus* is a small, shrubby plant with lemon-scented leaves up to ½ in. long and tiny pale lilac flowers in clusters on the tips of the branches during summer. *T.* x *c.* 'Aureus' has golden leaves tinged with green, and *T.* x *c.* 'Silver Queen' has silver and green variegated leaves. Propagate by taking semiripe cuttings in summer.

Viola tricolor
H 5 in. S 6 in.
Sun/partial shade
Moderate
Any Z4

The Johnny-jump-up or heartsease is a small, tuft-forming annual, biennial, or short-lived perennial ideal for a border or container. It has toothed, heart-shaped leaves and pretty, delicately scented three-colored flowers during spring, summer, and into fall. Of the five petals, the upper two are dark purple or violet, the central two paler purple, and the bottom one yellow streaked with violet. The colors are not definite, and the middle petals may be almost white or as dark as purple. The form 'Bowles' Black' is very deep violet with a yellow eye. This plant is short-lived (from seeds sown in spring) but sets seeds easily and may be invasive.

ANNUALS & BIENNIALS

Calendula officinalis 'Fiesta Gitana'
H 12 in. S 12 in.
Sun/partial shade
Well-drained/moderate
Any Z8

This pot marigold is a compact, fast-growing annual plant with multiple stems and lancelike, hairy, aromatic foliage. Throughout summer and fall, it produces daisylike double flowers in shades of orange and yellow with darker orange centers. Use this plant for an added splash of color at the front of a border, or in a container or window box. Regular deadheading will keep it from setting seeds and will ensure a continuous succession of flowers. Any seed that does form and is shed is likely to grow the following year. Propagate by sowing seeds in the final growing position in late spring.

Datura inoxia
H 3 ft. S 4 ft.
Sun
Moderate
Any Z9

Commonly called the thorn apple, this half-hardy annual originates from central South America. It is grown for its exceptional display of 12-in., white, heavily scented, trumpet-shaped flowers. These pendulous flowers are produced singly or in groups of three during the summer months and open in the evening. The large evergreen leaves, up to 10–12 in. in length, are oblong with an elongated point. They are a mid-green color with wavy margins and are covered with a coating of soft, feltlike hairs. Propagate by taking semiripe heel cuttings in early summer.

Heliotropium arborescens
H 18 in. S 16 in.
Sun
Moderate
Any Z10

This tender evergreen shrub is usually grown as an annual for display purposes. The thick, textured, wrinkled leaves are dark green in color and oblong in shape. They are carried on dark green, almost black, stems. The small flowers are formed in 4-in., flat clusters and are very fragrant, with colors varying from a deep bluish-purple to lavender and pure white. Some types can be raised from seeds, including the newer 'Mini Marine,' with its compact, bushy habit, bronze-green leaves, and violet-purple flowers. Propagate by taking cuttings in autumn or sowing seeds in spring.

ANNUALS & BIENNIALS

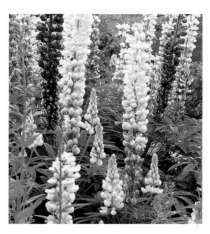

Limnanthes douglasii
H 6 in. S 10 in.
Sun
Moderate
Any Z8

This hardy annual is a low-growing plant with thin, creeping stems covered in bright green leaves with a lightly toothed margin. It spreads by self-seeding. It is grown for its sweetly scented, saucer-shaped flowers, which have yellow centers and a white margin to each petal, giving it the common name of poached eggplant. It is ideal for attracting beneficial insects into the garden because, in addition to its scent, it also produces nectar to attract bees and butterflies. In mild, sheltered places, this plant can survive outdoors over winter. Propagate by sowing seeds in early to late spring.

Lobularia maritima
H 6 in. S 9 in.
Sun
Moderate
Any Z7

This member of the cabbage family originates from the Canary Islands. It is a low-growing annual with a spreading, branching habit and slightly hairy, gray-green leaves that are narrow, straplike, and up to 1 in. long. Throughout summer, tiny, cross-shaped, sweetly fragrant flowers are produced in clusters often reaching 3 in. across. These blooms are usually pure white or occasionally pinkish-white or purple. Deadheading the flowers will encourage the production of a second display of flowers later. Propagate by sowing seeds in the final growing position in late spring.

Lupinus luteus
H 30 in. S 12 in.
Sun
Moderate
Acid/neutral Z6

This striking annual plant has mid-green stems, thickly covered with soft, slender hairs. The pale to mid-green, broadly oval leaves are narrower toward the base and sparsely covered in a coating of fine, soft, shaggy hair. In midsummer, bright yellow flowers with the scent of vanilla are arranged in a circle or whorl at the end of the stem. In the autumn, these are followed by small, black, hairy pods, each containing an average of five slightly flattened black seeds. Propagate by sowing seeds in the final growing position in spring; presoak the seed in water for twenty-four hours.

ANNUALS & BIENNIALS

Matthiola incana
H 6–30 in. S 9–12 in.
Sun
Moderate
Alkaline/neutral Z6

There are various forms of stock, most of which are grown as annuals, although some are perennial if they are left to grow. They have gray-green leaves and flower profusely through the summer in upright spikes of fragrant purple, violet, mauve, pink, or white double or single blooms. There are many seed mixes, in various heights and multiple colors, including 'Cinderella' (spicy, clove scent, double, dwarf), 'Legacy' (long flowering season, double, strongly fragrant), and 'Ten Week Mixed' (compact, highly fragrant, quick-growing annual). Propagate by sowing seeds in summer for the longest flowering season the following year, overwintering under cover to prevent fungal attack.

Mirabilis jalapa
H 3 ft. S 3 ft.
Sun
Well-drained
Any Z8

This is a bushy tender perennial plant (often grown as an annual) with broadly oval, mid-green leaves arranged in opposite pairs on fleshy green stems, often with dark red or purple markings around the leaf joints. The large, trumpet-shaped flowers are white, yellow, red, or magenta and open in the afternoon, hence the common name of four-o'clock flower. They are heavily fragrant and are at their most scented in the evening. They die by morning to be replaced by more flowers the following afternoon. Propagate by sowing seeds outdoors in late spring or by dividing in spring.

Nicotiana x _sanderae_
H 10–24 in. S 12–18 in.
Sun
Moderate
Any Z7

This ornamental relative of tobacco is a multibranched and stout-stemmed plant that grows as an annual, biennial, or sometimes short-lived perennial, according to the conditions. The wavy-edged leaves grow as a basal rosette, from which the tall flowering stem rises. The individual flowers have a tube up to 3½ in. long, flaring into a wide trumpet shape with five rounded lobes. They are available in white and shades of red, pink, purple, and even lime-green, and they release their scent in the evening. Propagate by sowing seeds in spring as summer bedding in a border or in a container. Compact forms, such as 'Domino Mixed,' are ideal for a container.

Pelargonium

H 6–24 in. S 6–24 in.
Sun/partial shade
Well-drained/moderate
Any Z10

Geraniums are grown for their bright, attractive flowers and/or their scented foliage. Regal cultivars are evergreen perennials with thick, branching stems, hairy, toothed, palmlike leaves, and large flowers in white, pink, salmon, orange, red, or purple. Scented-leaf forms have smaller flowers and finely cut, toothed, or finely lobed foliage with a lemon, peppermint, orange, lime, or balm scent. Zonal geraniums have smooth, succulent stems and large, rounded leaves. The flowers may be single, semidouble, or double in white, orange, pink, red, purple, and yellow. Trailing forms have ivylike foliage and single or double flowers in white, purple, red, pink, and mauve. Propagate by tip cuttings from nonflowering shoots in early or late summer.

Petunia

H 12 in. S 12–36 in.
Sun
Moderate
Any Z7

Although many petunias are herbaceous perennials, they are treated as half-hardy annuals that flower in the first season from seeds and are one of the most popular plants for hanging baskets, tubs, and window boxes. They are colorful plants and come in white and shades of cream, pink, red, mauve, blue, and a variety of striped forms, most with a vanilla fragrance, especially at night. The leaves, carried on green, hairy stems, are broadly oval, mid- to dark green in color, and sticky to the touch. Deadhead the flowers regularly to keep the plants flowering continually. Propagate by sowing seeds in spring.

Phacelia tanacetifolia

H 4 ft. S 18 in.
Sun
Well-drained
Any Z10

This is a hardy annual originating from the southwestern United States and Mexico. The mid-green leaves are about 10 in. long but are divided into large numbers of smaller, subdivided leaflets that are broadly lance-shaped. The entire surface of the plant is covered with a layer of short hairs, and contact with the skin may aggravate skin allergies. The blue or lavender-blue bell-shaped flowers are held above the leaves in dense, curved clusters and emit a strong heliotrope fragrance from midsummer through autumn. Propagate by sowing seeds in the final growing position in early spring or autumn.

ANNUALS & BIENNIALS

Phlox drummondii
H 4–24 in. S 12 in.
Sun
Moderate
Any Z6

The half-hardy annual phlox is grown for its attractive, brightly colored, fragrant flowers. They may be single or double, in white or shades of purple, red, pink, or lilac, and are carried in dense clusters up to 3 in. across on the tips of the shoots from mid- to late summer. It has an upright habit and narrow, straplike leaves of mid- to light green, carried in pairs on slender green stems. Available forms include named cultivars such as 'Double Chanel' (rich pale pink, double) and mixed-color seed collections such as 'Tapestry' (rich violet, yellow, salmon, pink and red). Deadhead regularly for continuous flowering. Propagate by sowing seeds in spring.

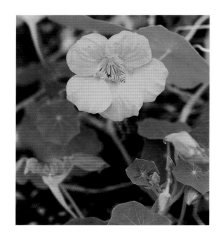

Tropaeolum majus
H 5 ft. S 5 ft.
Sun
Moderate
Any Z8

This is a climbing or trailing hardy annual with rounded, light green leaves, sometimes marked with white splashes. The long-spurred, broadly trumpet-shaped flowers are about 2 in. across and are borne throughout summer and fall in shades of yellow, cream, orange, and red, often with a contrasting splash in the throat. The scented flowers are edible and look colorful in a salad. There are many seed mixes available, including 'Trailing Mixed,' 'Out of Africa' (white-marbled leaves), and 'Gleam Mixed' (less vigorous, to 15 in.). Grow in containers, hanging baskets, or at the front of a border. Propagate by sowing seeds in spring (indoors, or outdoors once the risk of frost has passed).

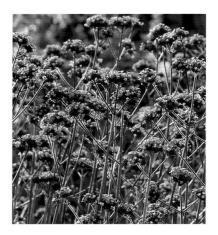

Verbena bonariensis
H 36 in. S 18 in.
Sun
Moderate
Any Z9

Usually grown as an annual, this verbena will overwinter in milder areas or in a frost-free greenhouse to form a clump-forming perennial. The tall, branching, wiry stems bear a few oblong to lance-shaped leaves and are topped by flattened clusters of tiny lilac-purple flowers from mid-summer to early autumn. The flowers have a delicate fragrance and are particularly attractive to butterflies. Deadhead in late summer to extend flowering. It will selfseed or can be propagated by sowing seed in fall or spring (sow under cover in cold areas), or by dividing in spring.

Aponogeton distachyos
H 4–6 in. S. 4 ft.
Sun/partial shade
Water
Z9

The water hawthorn is a moderately vigorous, aquatic perennial that, in most winters, remains evergreen. Its mid-green, oblong-shaped leaves have maroon markings and float on the water surface from a submerged rhizome. Clusters of small, hawthorn-scented flowers are carried on forked branches just above the water from spring right through to fall. Each small, white blossom has purple-black stamens at its base and is wrapped by a white spathe. Grow in soil or planting baskets at the bottom of water 12–36 in. deep. Because the rhizome is almost impossible to divide, propagate by dividing clumps during the growing season or by sowing seeds as soon as it is ready.

Iris pseudacorus
H 3 ft. S 10 in.
Sun/partial shade
Moist
Any Z5

Commonly called the yellow flag, this is a vigorous and extremely hardy true water iris (although it will grow in a border). It is easy to grow, often forming large clumps of tall, deciduous, blue-green, straplike leaves with pronounced ribs running the full length of each leaf. Tall, erect, green branching stems carry at least five bright yellow, scented blossoms with small black or chocolate brown markings during summer. The form I. p. 'Variegata' has yellow stripes running along the foliage. Propagate by sowing seeds in spring and early summer or by dividing immediately after flowering.

Nymphaea
H 2 in. S 16 in.–10 ft.
Sun
Water
Z3–10

The water lily is the queen of aquatic plants and ranges in size from small to enormous. Small varieties will fit in a bowl or waterproof container; large ones need a pond. These deciduous, herbaceous perennials produce dark green or bronze-tinted, circular, floating leaves, followed by open, starlike, sometimes scented flowers in colors from white to shades of yellow, pink, orange, and red. The flowers and leaves rise from a thick rootstock anchored securely in the soil base or in a planting basket. Fragrant forms include 'Caroliniana Rosea' (soft-pink flowers), 'Marliacea Albida' (white, flushed pink outside), and N. odorata types. Propagate by lifting and dividing the rootstocks in spring.

chapter five

5

Plants for fall

There are some plants that only really come into their own in the fall, such as the fern-leaf clematis (*Clematis cirrhosa*), which will actually start to flower as the days shorten. A number of herbaceous plants also provide their best display of fragrance and color at this time of year. Other plants will only consider flowering once they have shed their leaves, and some evergreens begin to produce deeply fragrant flowers that are barely visible under the canopy of thick, leathery leaves. Fall is also a good time for displays of bulbs, even though they are a group of plants more commonly associated with spring. Carpets of scented blooms look spectacular, especially under trees or in partially shaded areas where the fragrance lingers.

Trees

One notable plant for this time of year is the deciduous tree *Cercidiphyllum japonicum*, whose leaves provide outstanding autumn colors, with tints of orange, red, and even pink before turning butter-yellow. The real bonus with this tree is that, as the leaves change color, they release the aroma of hot sugar, resulting in the common name of cotton-candy tree. Other trees, such as *Prunus subhirtella* 'Autumnalis Rosea,' will start to flower soon after shedding their leaves, producing clouds of tiny almond-scented blossoms throughout the fall, winter, and early spring.

When the leaves begin to fall, it also allows more light into the shaded areas under the trees, encouraging plants such as *Cyclamen* to emerge and flower. Any plants beneath trees often have their highest light levels at this time of year, having been dormant through the summer when the soil was dry and shaded.

Climbers and wall shrubs

There are several interesting fragrant climbers that flower at this time. The sweetly scented *Clematis rehderiana* flowers in early fall, followed by the later-flowering *Clematis flammula*, with its hint of hawthorn fragrance. *Lonicera japonica* has lemon-scented flowers until midautumn, often later in a mild year, and *Jasminum officinale* will still produce sweetly scented white flowers until the frosts stop it.

Wall shrubs for fall include *Ceanothus* 'Gloire de Versailles,' with its pale blue flowers giving a sweet scent that will waft in through an open window on a warm day. The season can last slightly longer with these plants because some extra warmth is provided by the residual heat from the wall or fence.

Shrubs

Some of the fragrant plants that flower in the fall have an air of mystery about them. *Elaeagnus* x *ebbingei* has small, heavily fragrant flowers that are so well hidden by the tough, leathery leaves that it is the nose rather than the eye that leads you to the flower. Other deciduous shrubs with fragrant flowers that carry on into the fall include *Buddleia davidii*, with its minute tubular flowers whose fragrance acts like a magnet to butterflies. Its close relative *Buddleia fallowiana* will also still be flowering into the first half of autumn.

The pretty white and yellow flowers of Romneya coulteri *will bloom in autumn and perfume the air with their sweet scent.*

Bulbs and corms

Many bulbs and corms flower at this time of year. They have lain dormant during the warmer months but start to emerge in early autumn and produce flowers. *Cyclamen hederifolium* and *Crocus sativus* carry a mild scent and are best mass-planted in order to appreciate their fragrance because they are so low-growing. Some of the most strongly scented lilies continue to flower into the fall, including *Lilium auratum*, *L. henryi*, and *L. speciosum*, whose heady scent you can usually smell long before they come into view. These can therefore be planted more sparsely while still producing plenty of fragrance in the garden.

Annuals and biennials

Although most plants will be coming to the end of their life cycle, some will continue to produce flowers right up until the first frosts. Evening scents can be prominent at this time of the year, with *Oenothera biennis* and *Nicotiana sylvestris* producing their rich, sweet fragrance as the temperature falls and the daylight fades, drawing moths for pollination.

Perennials

A large number of perennials naturally flower in the second half of the year, providing color and scent into the fall. Plants such as *Gladiolus callianthus* 'Murieliae' and *Romneya coulteri*, both with white, sweetly scented flowers, and a number of different types of *Phlox* also flower in autumn, with *P. maculata* and *P. paniculata* producing flowers that are both attractive and fragrant.

Many herbaceous perennial plants that are left in position all year round will continue flowering well into the fall, stopping only when the first hard frosts turn the foliage black, marking the end of another year of growth and causing the plants to die back down to ground level.

Autumn weather and its effects

The weather can be erratic in the fall, with warm, sunny days, cool nights, and damp humidity, as well as wind and rain. The only constant is that the days are getting shorter, a fact that is responsible for major changes within the plants, both visible and unseen. Some of these changes will result in in deciduous plants shedding their leaves and a toughening of their cells to help them cope with the cold weather of the oncoming winter. The changes can be deceptive, for although many plants appear to be approaching dormancy, they do not actually rest completely until well into the depths of winter.

Jobs for fall

As the heat of summer begins to wane, autumn is a time of mellow days and golden light. Much of the fall is spent tidying the garden as plant growth gradually slows down, but many of the tasks carried out now not only clear away the evidence of one growing season but are equally important in preparing the garden for the next. Autumn is a time of balance between the summer past and the winter ahead, so it is the ideal season to make plans for the following year's garden. Learn from this year's successes and failures, and use the lessons to plan future gardening projects. If you are eager to experiment, collect seed catalogs and select some new cultivars of seeds or plants to try out. This will create added interest as well as introduce new fragrances into areas of the garden or indoors.

Mulching

Applying a mulch to the soil in autumn can benefit plants considerably, especially if the mulch is an organic one. The soil is still warm from the summer, so applying a covering now will keep this residual heat trapped in the soil for a longer period. Although this will not extend the growing period of the plants, their root development can continue for several more weeks so that they gain a slightly earlier start the following spring. If the mulch is applied just after they shed their leaves and all of the fallen leaves are cleared away, the spores of fungal diseases such as rose black spot that overwinter on the soil are suppressed.

Insulating containers

Plants growing in containers will need some protection over the coming months because the roots are the part most vulnerable to frost damage. Some form of insulation material, such as bubble wrap or horticultural fleece, would certainly improve the plants' chances of survival. Wrap the material loosely around the containers (not the plants) so that a layer of air between the container and the wrapping provides additional insulation.

Support structures

Many plants, especially those with long trailing growths, are susceptible to physical damage as the weather becomes more unsettled and the winds become stronger. Climbers and wall shrubs suffer more damage from poor or inadequate tying and support than from any form of pest or disease, and most of the damage occurs in fall and winter. During early to midautumn, tie in any new shoots that are to be kept and check the ties on old established growths to make sure they are not cutting into stems and branches. Replace any worn ties and strings. If the support structure for these plants is damaged, tie the long, straggly growths of the plants into loose bunches, and, after the leaves fall, replace or repair the supports before spreading the growths out and tying them into position.

Any young trees that have stakes and ties should be checked to make sure that the stake is in a sound, firm condition to keep the root system stable in windy conditions. Tree ties should be examined to make sure they are not frayed or worn and that they are not constricting the stem of the tree in any way.

The Mexican orange (Choisya ternata) *produces musk-scented flowers from late summer to fall. Remove the dead flower heads in late autumn to ensure another good display the following spring.*

Autumn is the time to harvest seeds from flowers such as the flowering tobacco (Nicotiana alata).

Deadheading

As plants gradually finish flowering, remove the dead flower heads. Some can be saved and used in potpourri (see page 30), such as the old flowers of the bee balm (*Monarda didyma*). Deadheading in early fall will encourage plants to produce a few more late flowers or to hang on to their flowers slightly longer, whereas deadheading in late fall will keep the plants tidy and reduce the amount of damage done to the base of the plant as the stems rock in the winter winds.

Harvesting

This time of year is always associated with harvesting (see pages 28–31). Many plants, such as *Amberboa mochata* and *Nicotiana alata*, will have produced seeds that need to be harvested to form the basis of the following year's design. Mark the best plants when they flower to be sure only their seed is saved. Wait until the seed heads are just about to split before harvesting them and laying them in trays or on sheets of paper in a dry, cool room to allow the seeds to emerge naturally. All collected seeds should be stored in labeled, airtight containers in a cool, dark place. Replace harvested plants with some that will provide displays of color and fragrance during late winter and early spring.

Propagation & planting

Many late summer–flowering plants will continue to provide color and fragrance well into the fall mists as the flowers make one last effort to produce seeds. The leaves may be colorful and the air sweet with the scent of ripe fruit, but far from a state of happy complacency, you should be preparing for the following year to ensure that everything is ready for another glorious display once the colder months are over. This is the time of year to take out winter insurance, propagating any plants that are marginally hardy and may succumb to a very cold or wet winter, giving you backup for the following spring if required. The soil is still warm in autumn, so it is also an ideal time for introducing some new plants into the garden. These will be in good condition to get off to a quick start the following spring as the soil begins to warm up again.

Seedlings

Sweet peas (*Lathyrus odoratus*) can be sown in pots of loam-based compost in autumn and grown in a cold frame over the winter. These can be transplanted outdoors during late spring the following year. For maximum scent, choose old-fashioned cultivars such as 'Cupani' and 'Painted Lady.' This is also a good time of year to collect and sow the seeds of woody plants. This should be done just before the seeds and fruits are fully ripe. Plants such as roses (*Rosa*) produce their seeds inside a fleshy hip or berrylike fruit. Separate the seed from this outer coating before sowing. Other plants, such as fernleaf maple (*Acer japonicum* and *A. palmatum*), produce dry fruits that can be sown in the garden directly after collection.

Cuttings

Marginally hardy and some hardy plants can be propagated from semiripe cuttings in the fall before the frosts. Alternatively, many trees and shrubs can be propagated at this time of year from hardwood cuttings.

Semiripe cuttings

Take semiripe cuttings (an intermediate growth stage between softwood and hardwood) from the tips of marginally hardy plants such as sage (*Salvia officinalis*), French lavender (*Lavandula stoechas*), and *Penstemon*. Grow them in a cold frame or unheated greenhouse until they have rooted, and root them in a slightly dry atmosphere to ensure that they do not rot. Many aromatic plants that have silver leaves hail from Mediterranean regions and succumb to the combination of cold and wet conditions rather than just low temperatures. Hardy plants such as *Mahonia*, *Osmanthus*, and *Skimmia* can also be propagated from semiripe cuttings, but they need a more humid environment to keep them alive until they form roots.

Hardwood cuttings

Trees and shrubs such as the mock orange (*Philadelphus*), clove currant (*Ribes odoratum*), and *Viburnum farreri* will all root from hardwood cuttings taken from the current season's growth. These plants can be rooted out in the garden and will need no protection over the winter. Even though no leaves will develop until spring, they will often form new roots by midwinter and will be suitable for planting out within a year.

Take hardwood cuttings from shrubs such as the mock orange (Philadelphus) *during autumn. They can be planted out within a year.*

Bulbs

Early fall is also the ideal time for planting many of the spring-flowering bulbs. In the warm, moist soil, they will start to produce roots within a few weeks of being planted, even though it may be several months before any leaves become visible above ground. Scented *Narcissus* such as 'Bunting,' 'Cheerfulness,' 'Quail,' 'Old Pheasant's Eye,' and 'Queen Anne's Jonquil' are ideal for naturalizing and provide plenty of fragrance from early spring until early May.

Fragrant bulbs that are to be used for indoor displays, such as tulips (*Tulipa*) and hyacinths (*Hyacinthus*), can be potted now and prepared for "forcing" (see pages 62–63), ready to provide scent and color from midwinter through to early spring. Lily of the valley (*Convallaria majalis*) can be induced to flower by midwinter, and varieties of *Narcissus*, which hardly need any forcing at all, can be potted up in the fall to be in flower throughout late winter and early spring.

Trees and shrubs

Autumn is an excellent time for planting shrubs, conifers, and trees while the soil is still warm. The roots will have several weeks to begin to establish, even after the top of the plant has become dormant. This will not only help it survive the winter but will also give it a head start in spring because it will be ready to grow as soon as the temperatures begin to rise. Trees that are planted now should be firmly staked, because the windiest time of the year is approaching. Climbers and wall shrubs should be either tied to a support system or pruned back to prevent any loosening of the roots or damage to branches and stems as a result of "windrock."

This is a good time of year to plant conifers or broad-leaved evergreens because they go through a burst of growth in early autumn. However, they must have some protection from strong winds that may draw moisture from the foliage before the new roots have established, which in turn could cause drying of the leaves, making them turn brown.

Fall is also an ideal time to plant hedge shrubs (see pages 144–45) that will act as windbreaks to protect the more vulnerable plants in the garden from wind damage. The hedge will filter the wind and cause less turbulence than a solid barrier, such as a wall. Mixed-variety—or "tapestry"—hedges look wonderful and can be a source of color and fragrance through the changing seasons.

Mediterranean border

Many fragrant plants originate from countries where temperatures are quite hot at certain times of the year. In fact, some plants with aromatic foliage, such as lavender (*Lavandula*) and *Nepeta*, even produce stronger scents as temperatures rise. These plants lend themselves to cultivation on a hot, sunny site, especially where the soil is light, sandy, and particularly free-draining. A striking Mediterranean-style border can be created by growing a selection of plants with contrasting aromatic leaves.

WHAT YOU NEED

Tools: Spade, knife, trowel, wheelbarrow, garden fork
Materials: Landscape fabric; container-grown plants such as *Artemisia*, *Cistus ladanifer*, *Cordyline australis*, *Lavandula angustifolia*, and *Santolina chamaecyparissus*; pebble/slate mulch

In a warm, sunny site, it makes sense to use some form of mulch over the border soil to help suppress both weed growth (by keeping light from reaching the soil) and the amount of water being lost from the soil due to evaporation. Materials such as gravel, rocks, and different grades of pebbles have become very popular as a means of covering the soil and reducing garden maintenance. Gray or blue slate chips can also be used as an alternative to pebbles, providing an attractive contrast to the plants' foliage. Cover the soil with a water-permeable sheet or membrane, such as woven black plastic, before the stones are laid to reduce the quantity of stones needed, to provide an adequate covering to control weeds, and to limit evaporation.

The plants selected for this style of border must be carefully chosen to cope with particularly warm, dry conditions (the heat reflected from the stones will also increase temperatures by creating a very hot microclimate). The best plants to choose are therefore those with leaves adapted to cope with bright, sunny conditions. This includes plants with silver or gray foliage, a covering of felt or hairs over the leaf surface, or long, straplike leaves.

> **Tip:** To avoid swamping smaller plants, cover them with an overturned plant pot before spreading the mulching material, then remove the pot—this is easier than having to pick gravel or chips out of the plants' foliage.

Start by clearing and leveling the area before planting begins. Place a sheet of heavy-gauge landscape fabric over the bed and seal the edges by tucking them in at least 6 in. deep, stretching the fabric as tightly as possible.

Using the heel of your boot or shoe, firmly close the groove in the soil that is holding the landscape fabric.

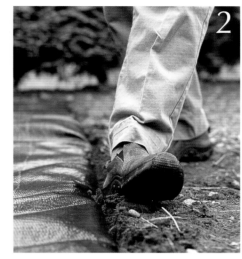

Using a sharp knife, cut a cross in the fabric at the point where each plant is to be placed, and fold back the flaps of plastic to reveal the soil beneath.

Use a trowel to dig out a planting hole large enough to accommodate the rootball of the plant that is about to be planted.

Holding the plant by its rootball, place it through the plastic into the hole. Using the trowel (or your hands, if you prefer), pull the soil back into the hole around the plant, and pack gently into place.

Fold the plastic flaps back into position around the base of the plant. Then tip piles of inorganic material—slate chips or gravel—onto the plastic around the base of the plants and spread them evenly. Ensure any remaining areas of plastic are completely covered with the stones.

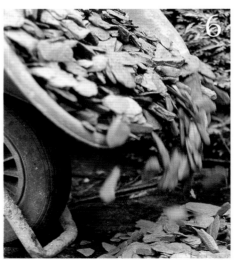

Scented seat

Almost everyone enjoys sitting out in the garden or sunbathing on a lawn. If you have a sloping garden, you can sit on a bank, but on a level site, it is possible to create a turf seat in the garden. By growing scented plants in parts of the seat, you can enjoy the feeling of grass beneath you, as well as the aroma of your favorite fragrant plants.

WHAT YOU NEED

Tools: Garden canes, string, rake, pressboard, large knife
Materials: Cardboard template (available from some garden centers or by mail order/Internet from some garden supply companies); bricks or rubble; good-quality soil; turf or grass seed; plants such as *Tanacetum vulgare*, *Tanacetum parthenium*, *Chamaemelum nobile*, and *Mentha* x *piperita citrata*

Herbs or low-growing plants could be used as an alternative to grass, but these plants tend not to be as hard-wearing and contain more sap than grass does, which means that light crushing as you sit can result in green stains on clothing. In order to blend fragrance with practicality, the bulk of the seat should be covered in grass to bind the structure together, with pockets of herbs planted at various places in the seat. The herbs will release aroma when brushed against while the seat is in use but pose no danger to clothing. Select plants that are able to tolerate clipping at roughly the same rate as the grass that covers the seat.

Herbs such as Roman chamomile (*Chamaemelum nobile*), lemon mint (*Mentha* x *piperita* var. *citrata*), and garden thyme (*Thymus vulgaris*) release aromatic oils that can have a very relaxing effect when drifting in the air close by. Other herbs, such as feverfew (*Tanacetum parthenium*), pennyroyal (*Mentha pulegium*), and common tansy (*Tanacetum vulgare*), are natural insect repellents and the aromas they release will help to ward off the biting and stinging insects that can be such persistent pests on a warm summer evening.

> **Tip:** It is important to remember that this type of seat will gradually settle as it becomes established. Allow for this settlement by constructing the seat slightly higher than you actually require it to be.

Mark a 5-ft.-diameter circle using canes and a length of string. This circle will form the base of the seat. Rake the area level and walk over it several times to compact the soil.

Assemble the cardboard template according to the manufacturer's instructions. Make sure that each section is firmly fixed to its adjoining sections so that the structure is stable.

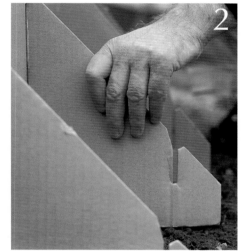

Fill each of the pockets in the template with bricks or rubble until the pockets are about two-thirds full. This packing material gives the seat structural strength when the cardboard decays and helps to improve drainage.

Fill the remaining portion of the pockets with good-quality soil and pat it down with a pressboard to firm it into place. If the soil is slightly moist, it will bond together more easily.

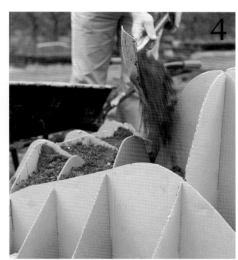

Lay sections of turf over the surface area of the seat and cut away any surplus turf so that a close fit can be achieved. Alternatively, sow grass seeds over the surface of the soil and allow it to germinate and grow.

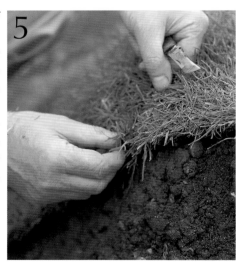

Plant scented plants into the arms of the chair. Select plants that are able to tolerate clipping at roughly the same rate as the grass that covers the seat.

Harvesting & drying flowers

Although plants are grown primarily to decorate the garden, the life of many flowers can be prolonged by storing them for use in dry displays to brighten up the house during winter. It is possible to preserve certain flowers so that they retain their natural fragrance as well as their form and color. The flower heads of lavender (*Lavandula*), which are used in this project, can retain their scent long after flowering has ended.

WHAT YOU NEED
Tools: Pruning shears, rubber bands, nails or hooks
Materials: Plants such as *Lavandula angustifolia*

Although the flower heads of some plants, such as *Allium*, will dry naturally if they are left on the plant, it can be an unsatisfactory process if they are battered by the weather. Much better results can be obtained if the heads are cut and preserved while they are in peak condition. Ideally, flowers should be cut on a fine, dry day just before they become fully open. Do not collect them when the air is damp or they are still covered with morning dew, because they will become moldy and discolored rather than dry properly.

Almost any flower can be air-dried, but some are more difficult than others. It is also a slow process, often taking several weeks. The best method involves hanging the flowers upside down in small, loose bunches (tied tightly at the base) in a dry, well-ventilated place. They should be kept out of direct sunlight, because the sun would cause the flowers to fade. After drying, the bunches can then be removed from the drying area, sorted and rebunched, and stored until needed by hanging them in a cool, dry place such as a garage or shed.

> **Tip:** Some species of lavender may shed their flowers as they dry. To avoid losing the flowers, place a paper bag over them while they are drying.

The lavender is ready to be cut when the flowers are half to three-quarters open. They will continue to open while they are drying.

Choose a warm, sunny day when the surface of the whole plant, particularly the flowers, is dry. This will prevent mold from developing. Cut the stems with sharp pruning shears to avoid bruising the stem or flower stalk.

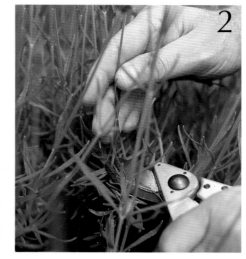

Working on a clean, flat surface, sort through the flower stalks, stripping off the leaves and discarding any bruised or broken stems.

Grade and sort the stems for size and length, gathering fifteen to twenty stems together. Tie them firmly with a rubber band. Do not use string because it would work loose as the stems dry and shrink.

Hang the complete bunches from nails or hooks in a dry, cool, dark place with good ventilation. Leave them for two to four weeks, depending on the plants being dried and how dry the atmosphere is.

When the stems are completely dry, sort through the bunches again and remove any withered flowers and stems before bunching the lavender into bouquets of about eighty to a hundred stems.

Naturalizing bulbs

Bulbs seldom grow individually in the wild but instead are found as clumps or carpets. There is no reason why we cannot imitate this in the garden, rather than planting them in regimented rows. Clumps of bulbs in a border or under a tree will create a natural effect as well as attract the eye. The fragrance will also be much stronger where flowers are massed together. The clump will need to be divided eventually, because as the bulbs reproduce and spread, they will begin to restrict each other. This can be done by lifting the entire clump after flowering as the foliage dies down and replanting it as several smaller clumps.

Bulb carpets

Carpets of bulbs can be planted wherever space allows. They look particularly good beneath deciduous trees, where they can flower while the tree is bare. This gives them the light levels they need to bloom, but they can lie dormant while the tree is in leaf and the light levels are low.

Aim to match the bulb to the situation to gain the best effect, using large flowers such as daffodils (*Narcissus*) where there is plenty of room—large flowers would be in scale in a large area, but they would dominate a small garden. Conversely, small flowers like *Crocus* are difficult to see in a large area but would be perfectly in scale with a small lawn.

Naturalizing in grass

If you decide to plant the bulbs to come up through grass, try to match the bulb to the conditions. Tiny bulbs will not have the ability to push their way through very coarse turf with thickly matted roots; in this instance, a large variety would stand a better chance of survival. Smaller bulbs are better suited to a fine grass mixture, which will have a less-dense root system.

Narcissus look delightful when naturalized in their surroundings and their fragrance will have a stronger impact if they are planted en masse.

Naturalizing in borders

Bulbs can be planted in borders to give a splash of color and fragrance whenever their surroundings need a boost. Spring bulbs, like *Narcissus*, will flower while deciduous shrubs are still leafless and before herbaceous perennials have begun the new season's growth. Summer bulbs, such as *Allium*, will complement surrounding flowers, adding an element of height to low plantings. Autumn-flowering bulbs, including *Cyclamen hederifolium*, *Colchicum*, and *Crocus tommasinianus*, lie dormant through the hot, dry months of summer, when the neighboring plants cast shade, and flower as the leaves fall and allow more light in.

Feeding

Remove the flowers as soon as they die (to keep seeds from setting) and begin to feed the bulbs with 1 oz. of potassium sulphate per square yard. This will help replenish the food the

bulb used in order to produce the flower. The leaves and remaining flower stem will continue to feed the bulb until the foliage dies down. Feeding before the flower fades makes the stem weak and floppy, ruining the flower.

Aftercare

It is important for the health of the bulbs that they are allowed to die down naturally after flowering, which takes six to eight weeks. This replenishes the food reserve within the bulb, preparing it to produce flowers for the following year. If this is not allowed to happen, the flowers will be of poorer quality or may not be present at all.

If you have planted bulbs in an area of turf, the grass among the leaves cannot be cut until the leaves have turned brown (keep this in mind when choosing where to plant your bulbs, because this may not be acceptable on a particularly fine lawn area). Once they have turned brown, the leaves can be removed by hand or mown off with the rest of the grass.

This onion-scented Allium christophii *seed head is growing in a patch of fennel* (Foeniculum vulgare), *which has an aniseed fragrance.*

Planting bulbs

Plant fragrant, spring-flowering bulbs in mid- to late autumn. The planting and aftercare of bulbs is relatively straightforward, but, contrary to popular belief, there is more to growing them than simply digging a hole in the soil and dropping a bulb into it. Attention to detail when planting is important and can mean the difference between success and failure.

WHAT YOU NEED
Tools: Bulb planting tool
Materials: Bulbs

The bulbs found in most gardens have been propagated in the same country or region as the garden. Some, however, may have originated from as far away as South Africa, South America, the Mediterranean, or the Middle East, and this will have an effect on the conditions the bulbs require in order to flourish. Start by selecting the right plant for your particular situation. Most bulbs prefer a sunny position, but a few, such as bluebells (*Hyacinthoides nonscripta*) and snowdrops (*Galanthus*), prefer the dappled shade provided by trees. Many bulbs are ideal for planting under deciduous trees because they are dormant when the trees are in full leaf, and flower when the trees are dormant and the light levels are better. Most soil types are suitable for the majority of bulbs, but try to ensure that the soil is not waterlogged during the winter, or the bulb may rot.

Planting depth is particularly important, because inconsistent planting will lead to uneven flowering, which can spoil the effect of mass groupings of bulbs. Depending on the bulbs being planted, the depth can vary from as shallow as ½ in. to as deep as 10 in. It is preferable to use some form of tool for making the planting hole, but because of the wide variation in planting depth, no single tool is ideal for all bulbs.

Tip: Bulbs that are naturalized in the lawn should be left for at least six weeks after flowering before you cut down the foliage. In the meantime, you will have to mow around them. To simplify this task, group the bulbs together so that there are fewer areas to mow around.

Scatter a handful of bulbs over the desired area. This will help you achieve a random, natural look that is particularly suitable for a group of bulbs growing in grass. Plant the bulbs where they land.

Push the bulb planting tool into the ground with a twisting motion (this is much easier than trying to force the planter into the ground vertically). Still twisting, pull the planter out of the ground, removing a core of soil with it.

You can use a hand bulb planter (as pictured in step 2), or, for harder ground, an upright spade-type bulb planter will make the work much easier.

Place the bulb into the hole in an upright position, but do not press it down too firmly, or, as the roots develop, they will push against the soil and force the bulb out of the ground.

Break up most of the core of the soil plug you removed in the bulb planting tool. Place the soil back in the hole around the bulb until it is level with the top of the bulb.

Place the remainder of the soil plug on top of the hole and press it gently into the ground using your boot.

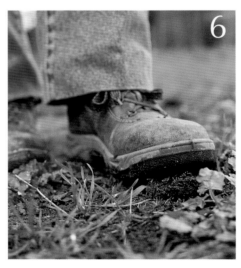

Fragrant hedges

Hedges can be used in a variety of ways around the garden to fulfill different functions, including marking boundaries, dividing the garden into sections, providing screens for increased privacy, and acting as a windbreak. If you are using container-grown plants such as lavender (*Lavandula*), the best times to plant are fall and spring. In autumn, the soil is still warm enough for the plant to make some root growth before it stops growing for the winter. In spring, the soil will be warming up again and the plant will soon begin to send out new roots. Bare-root plants, such as privet (*Ligustrum*), can be bought in bundles from late autumn until early spring and can be planted as soon as the weather allows.

Boundary demarcation

Hedges can be used to form a living barrier around the perimeter of your property. This may be preferable to having a solid boundary such as a wall or fence. Much will depend on your particular property and whether there are any restrictions on what can and cannot be built (check with your local authority). A hedge can be used in conjunction with a solid structure if, for instance, the wall is not as high as you would like.

Screening

If all or part of your garden is on view, a hedge may be the answer to gaining some privacy without building a solid barrier. A short, aromatic hedge around the sitting or dining area may be sufficient to create a feeling of privacy. You can also use hedging to hide parts of the garden that are less attractive, such as the area where you keep the trash cans or compost heap.

Wind protection

If your garden is subject to strong winds, your plants will not thrive. Even light winds can cause scorching and distorted or damaged growth. To appreciate the fragrance of the plants you are introducing, the air should be calm as often as possible. Solid barriers such as walls cause turbulence inside the garden because the wind is diverted over the top of the wall and then swirls down inside the garden. Hedges allow some of the wind to pass through so that the flow of air is reduced to manageable levels.

Dividing into sections

Low or medium hedges can be used to mark out different areas within the garden, edge paths, and guide people as they walk around. They can even be used to separate the garden into different sections, or "rooms," if the garden is large enough.

Growth habit

When you are planning the hedge, you need to decide whether it is to be formal or informal, in keeping with the rest of the design. This will influence which plant you can use in a particular situation, because the growth habit will dictate how it will respond to pruning. American boxwood (*Buxus sempervirens*) has a dense, twiggy habit and can be clipped into formal geometric shapes, whereas lavender (*Lavandula*) does not respond well to pruning and is better suited to informal hedging.

This clever design intersperses shaped hedging with areas of fragrant planting, creating both visual and aromatic interest.

Lavender (Lavandula) *has a bushy habit that makes it ideal for growing as a fragrant hedge in an informal-style garden.*

Pruning

If the hedge is being grown for its aromatic leaves, you can prune it regularly to reduce its size and maintain the shape of the hedge without affecting the production of fragrance. If the plants have been selected for their flowers, however, the timing of the pruning is much more critical so that you do not remove the buds or flowers before their best display. A plant such as *Chaenomeles* flowers in early spring and produces fragrant fruits in autumn, so it is best pruned right after flowering to allow it the full year to make more flowering growth. You will be sacrificing some fruits, but, over time, regular pruning will result in a bushy, dense plant that will fruit heavily.

Planting a fragrant hedge

Hedges serve all sorts of purposes within the garden—they make excellent screens and barriers, provide a habitat for birds and other wildlife, and serve as a natural backdrop for other plants in the garden. A number of coniferous plants with aromatic foliage are ideal for hedging and will provide fragrance when the weather is warm and particularly when the hedge is being trimmed.

WHAT YOU NEED
Tools: Garden line, measuring rod, spade, wheelbarrow
Materials: Conifer plants, organic mulch

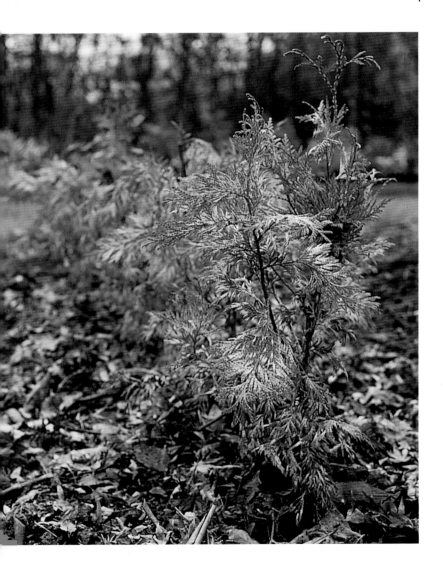

Coniferous evergreen plants are excellent for providing year-round shelter (particularly where walls and fences are not practical), as well as fragrance, when planted as hedging. Some, like *Thuja plicata* 'Zebrina,' have a sweet resinous aroma and the advantage of attractive green- and gold-variegated foliage; others, such as *Thuja occidentalis*, produce a resinous, pineapple scent.

The best time for planting depends on the plants being used. Deciduous plants are cheaper bought "bare-root" in bundles for planting between late fall and early spring, while broad-leaved evergreens and conifers are usually available as container-grown plants that can be planted in early fall or late spring.

Remember that a hedge is a long-term plant and that the soil should be well-prepared beforehand. The plants will need trimming regularly for the first few years to encourage the growth to become thick and bushy at the base.

Tip: To get the best effect from a fragrant hedge, grow it in a formal design, keeping it quite closely clipped to the desired height and outline. The hedging plants should be trimmed at least once a year, and more often (two or three times a year) with some of the more vigorous plants.

Start by marking out the course of the hedge with a garden line. To get accurate spacings between the plants, make a measuring rod, with the plant spacings marked on it from a section of wooden batten.

Using a spade, dig out the hole for the first plant, and place the soil in a wheelbarrow (this soil can be taken to the end of the hedge line and used to fill the final planting hole).

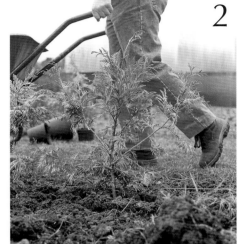

Remove the plant from its container and position it in the planting hole, making sure the rootball of the plant is at the correct height.

Dig out the hole for the second plant and put the soil from this second hole around the roots of the plant in the first planting hole.

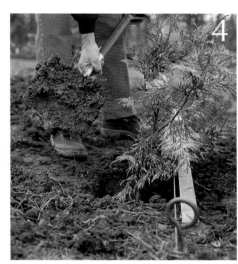

Adjust the level of the plant's roots (if necessary) and firm the soil in the planting hole with the heel of a boot or shoe. (Repeat steps 3, 4, and 5 until the hedge is completed).

Finally, remove the garden line and cover the soil with a layer of well-rotted organic mulch to suppress weeds and retain moisture.

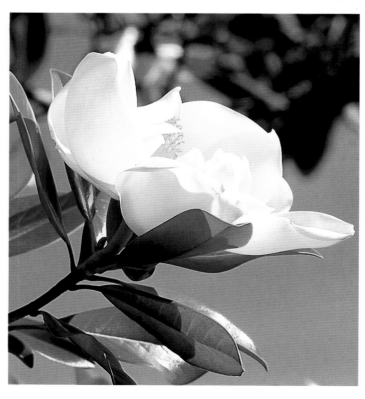

TREES

KEY INFORMATION

H: The average height the plant can reach

S: The average spread the plant can achieve

Sun/partial shade/shade:
The position the plant prefers

Well-drained/moderate/moist:
How much water the plant needs

Acid/alkaline/neutral/any:
The plant's preferred soil type

Z1 to Z10: The minimum winter temperature (zone) the plant can withstand

Zone 1: below –50°F
Zone 2: –50 to –40°F
Zone 3: –40 to –30°F
Zone 4: –30 to –20°F
Zone 5: –20 to –10°F
Zone 6: –10 to 0°F
Zone 7: 0 to 10°F
Zone 8: 10 to 20°F
Zone 9: 20 to 30°F
Zone 10: 30 to 40°F

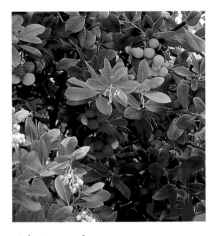

Arbutus unedo
H 26 ft. S 26 ft.
Sun
Moderate
Acid/neutral Z7

This attractive, slow-growing, broad-leaved evergreen forms an open, spreading, sometimes shrubby tree. It has deep brown bark that peels off to reveal the new green bark beneath. The white urn-shaped flowers are honey-scented and produced in large, hanging trusses on the tips of the branches in autumn. These are followed by orange-red fruits that take a year to ripen. There is also a form with dark pink flowers, *A. u. rubra*. Propagate by taking semiripe cuttings in late summer and placing them in a cold frame to root over winter.

Magnolia grandiflora
H 32 ft. S 16 ft.
Sun
Moderate
Acid/neutral Z6

This small tree is one of the best magnolias. The glossy evergreen leaves are up to 8 in. long and have an orange-brown, feltlike covering on the undersides. From midsummer until midautumn, large, bowl-shaped, creamy yellow flowers up to 10 in. across and with between nine and twelve petals are borne on the tips of shoots. The cultivar *M. g.* 'Exmouth' has richly fragrant flowers. Prune only to maintain the health and shape of the plant. Propagate by taking semiripe cuttings in summer or by layering shoots in autumn and severing them from the parent plant one or two years later.

Parrotia persica
H 26 ft. S 32 ft.
Sun/partial shade
Well-drained
Acid Z5

This small, deciduous tree is closely
related to *Hamamelis*. It has a
wide-spreading habit and is grown
mainly for its attractive autumn
leaf color. The leaves are roughly
oval in shape with a rounded base
and are mid-green in spring and
summer, turning crimson and
gold in autumn. Small, crimson,
delicately scented flowers appear in
late winter to early spring before the
leaves emerge. The bark of mature
plants flakes off in patches to reveal
interesting patterns in winter. There
is also a weeping form of this tree,
P. p. 'Pendula.' Propagate by taking
softwood cuttings in summer or
sowing seed in autumn.

Plumeria rubra
H 20 ft. S 15 ft.
Sun
Moderate
Any Z10

The common frangipani is a small,
deciduous tree with an upright
habit, consisting of a few sparse
but thick branches. It is ideal for
the sunroom, where its size can
be controlled by growing it in a
container. The mid-green leaves
are broadly lance-shaped and
arranged alternately along the stems.
In summer and fall, clusters of
strongly jasmine-scented, yellow-
eyed flowers are produced. The
flowers, which are up to 4 in. across
with rounded yellow, red, or bronze
petals, adopt a flat, open shape as
they develop. This plant can be
grown in a container and moved
indoors for winter protection.
Propagate by sowing seed at a
temperature of 64°F in the spring.

***Prunus subhirtella* 'Autumnalis Rosea'**
H 26 ft. S 26 ft.
Sun
Moderate
Any Z6

This deciduous tree has an open,
spreading habit and broadly oval-
shaped, dark green leaves with
sharply toothed margins; the leaves
are tinted purple when they emerge
in spring and turn a dull golden
yellow in autumn before they fall.
This remarkable tree hardly stops
flowering between autumn and
spring. The flowers fade and open
in steady succession, and there is
rarely a time when the tree does not
have some semidouble, rose-pink
flowers that carry a sweet almond
scent, although it is rarely totally
covered. Propagate by budding in
summer or grafting in winter.

SHRUBS

Abelia x grandiflora
H 10 ft. S 13 ft.
Sun
Moderate
Any Z5

This hybrid shrub of garden
origin has glossy, oval-shaped,
semievergreen leaves carried on
thin, twiggy branches, giving the
plant a loose, spreading appearance.
In late summer and throughout fall,
attractive tubular flowers are borne
in open clusters on the shoot tips.
They are lightly fragrant and
colored soft pink, fading to white
with age. A less vigorous form,
A. x grandiflora 'Francis Mason,'
is a better choice for smaller
gardens. Some protection may
be necessary in severe winters.
Propagate by taking 4-in. tip
cuttings in summer and placing
them in a cold frame.

Buddleia davidii
H 10 ft. S 16 ft.
Sun
Moderate
Any Z5

This vigorous shrub has an open,
spreading habit, producing long,
arching stems, and is commonly
known as the butterfly bush because
of the insects it attracts. The lance-
shaped, gray-green leaves are up to
10 in. long, with a light feltlike
covering when young. In late
summer through until late fall,
12-in. spikes of lilac to purple
or purple-red fragrant flowers
are produced on the tips of the
branches, followed by later, smaller
flowers from the lateral shoots.
There are a number of excellent
named cultivars, including 'Black
Knight' and 'Peace.' Propagate by
taking hardwood cuttings from
leafless stems in winter.

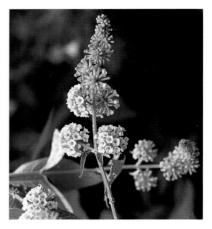

Buddleia x weyeriana 'Sungold'
H 12 ft. S 10 ft.
Sun
Moderate
Any Z6

A hybrid between B. davidii and
B. globosa, this deciduous shrub
has an open spreading habit. Its
arching brownish-green stems carry
opposite pairs of lance-shaped
silvery-green leaves, which are
covered in a dense grayish felt when
young. The tips of the stems bear
12-in.-long flower spikes with large
numbers of tiny fragrant flowers,
each with an orange center, which
open golden-yellow and fade to
yellowish-pink. Propagation is by
semiripe cuttings taken from side
shoots in the summer.

Choisya ternata
H 5 ft. S 5 ft.
Sun
Moderate
Any Z7

Elaeagnus x ebbingei
H 10 ft. S 10 ft.
Sun
Well-drained/moderate
Any Z6

Myrtus communis
H 10 ft. S 10 ft.
Sun
Well-drained/moderate
Any Z8

The Mexican orange is a compact, evergreen shrub with glossy, aromatic, palmate leaves produced in whorls on green, woody stems. Dense clusters of small, white, musk-scented, star-shaped flowers appear in late spring and again in late summer and autumn. *C. t.* 'Sundance' rarely flowers but has bright yellow foliage (although this may scorch in intense sunlight and turns lime-green in partial shade). *C.* 'Aztec Pearl' is compact with long, thin, dark green leaflets and pink-tinted, white flowers. Grow in any well-drained soil or a container, and prune only to remove any damaged shoots. Propagate by taking semiripe cuttings in late summer.

This is an attractive, hardy, and reliable evergreen shrub, tolerant of coastal exposure, with a spreading habit and scaly, golden bronze shoots. The leathery, broadly lance-shaped leaves are metallic green above and silvery green beneath. In fall and winter, small, highly fragrant, bell-like, white flowers are produced beneath the leaves. The fragrance is often noticed before the flowers are seen. Variegated cultivars include 'Gilt Edge' (yellow-edged leaves) and 'Limelight' (silvery new shoots and lime-green to yellow leaf markings). Remove any shoots that revert to green on a variegated plant, or they will take over. Propagate by taking semiripe cuttings in summer.

The myrtle is a bushy shrub with dense foliage and an upright habit, with the branches arching as the plant ages. The oval, aromatic leaves are glossy dark green and about 2 in. long, arranged in opposite pairs along orange-brown stems. From late summer into fall, the five-petaled white flowers have a pronounced central tuft of stamens and are sweetly scented. They are borne singly on the branches and are often followed by strongly aromatic, purple-black fruit in late autumn. Propagate by taking semiripe cuttings in late summer or sowing seeds in a cold frame in autumn.

SHRUBS

Osmanthus armatus
H 16 ft. S 13 ft.
Sun/partial shade
Well-drained
Any Z7

This is a rounded shrub with a
dense habit, often spreading with
age. It has large, lance-shaped,
evergreen leaves with a sharp,
spiny-toothed margin. The leaves
are a shiny dark green with a tough,
leathery texture, measuring up to
6 in. in length. The creamy white,
broadly tubular flowers are very
sweetly scented and carried in
clusters at the base of each leaf
joint on young branching stems
in autumn. The flowers are often
followed by 1-in.-long, oval-shaped
berries that are dark violet in color.
Propagate by sowing seeds in a cold
frame as soon as it is ripe or by
taking semiripe cuttings in summer.

Osmanthus heterophyllus
H 16 ft. S 16 ft.
Sun/partial shade
Moderate
Any Z6

Originated in Japan, this slow-
growing shrub with a rounded,
spreading habit is often mistaken
for holly. The mid-green leaves have
a leathery texture and are broadly
elliptical in shape, about 2½ in.
long, with a row of spines along the
margin. The leaves are often absent
on the new stems of mature plants.
In early fall, small, fragrant, tubular
flowers are produced in small
clusters in the axils of the leaves
and stem, followed by oval, bluish-
black fruit. Both gold- and silver-
variegated forms are available.
Propagate by sowing seeds in a cold
frame as soon as it is ripe or by
taking semiripe cuttings in summer.

Yucca gloriosa
H 8 ft. S 7 ft.
Sun
Well-drained/moderate
Neutral Z7

A native of the southeastern United
States, this striking hardy evergreen
shrub thrives in poor, sandy
conditions. The long, straplike
leaves are a bluish-green in color,
maturing to dark green. They are
usually dried and brown at the tip
to form a sharp, spinelike point. In
late summer and into autumn, the
spectacular flower spikes are often
8 ft. high and covered with white,
drooping, bell-shaped, lilylike
blooms, each up to 2 in. long. The
cultivar *Y. g.* 'Nobilis' often has red
markings on the petals. Propagate
by removing and planting rooted
suckers in spring.

CLIMBERS & WALL SHRUBS

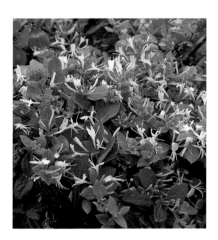

Lonicera japonica
H 32 ft. S 32 ft.
Sun/partial shade
Well-drained/moderate
Any Z4

This attractive Japanese honeysuckle has twining stems with evergreen to semievergreen leaves that are broadly oval in shape, glossy green in color, and carried in pairs on thin, twiggy stems. The fragrant flowers are tubular, opening out to a broad mouth, and are carried individually or in small clusters. They are a purple-tinged white when they first appear and age to a deep yellow. By late autumn, as the flowers fade, small blue to black fruits are produced. Prune by cutting back lateral shoots in spring and remove some of the older wood to allow room for younger shoots to develop. Propagate by taking hardwood cuttings in winter.

Passiflora caerulea
H 22 ft. S 16 ft.
Sun
Well-drained/moderate
Any Z7

The passionflower is a climbing perennial that will die down for the winter in all but the mildest areas and emerge as vigorous as ever the following spring. From late summer into fall, the beautiful large, fragrant flowers are borne singly on short green stalks. They have large pink-white sepals and petals, with spiky blue filaments tinged white and purple in the center of the bloom. The palm-shaped leaves have five to seven fingers, are mid-green in color, and are carried on square, green stems. The plant supports itself by using thin green tendrils and can grow up to 22 ft. in length within a season. Propagate by taking heel cuttings in mid- to late summer.

Rosa 'Mermaid'
H 23 ft. S 23 ft.
Sun
Moderate
Any Z5

One of the most useful and beautiful climbing roses, this vigorous plant has long, arching stems. The large, glossy green leaves are practically evergreen, carried on brownish-maroon wood and well armed with large, curved thorns, red when young and turning brown with age. The large, single, primrose-yellow flowers are often 4 in. across when fully open, revealing a huge cluster of golden-brown stamens in the center of each bloom. These fragrant flowers are produced from midsummer until well into autumn, stopping only when the first frosts arrive. Propagate by budding in summer or grafting in winter.

PERENNIALS, ANNUALS, & BIENNIALS

Achillea filipendulina
H 4 ft. S 18 in.
Sun
Moderate
Any Z3

Commonly known as fernleaf yarrow, this herbaceous perennial has a compact, upright habit with broad, finely divided, slightly hairy leaves that are a dull green in color. The lemon-yellow flowers are held erect above the foliage in bold, flat clusters 5–6 in. across from late summer until early fall. One very popular form is *A. f.* 'Gold Plate,' which has deep golden-yellow flowers. The finely cut foliage has a pungent aroma (feverfew) and is excellent for use in potpourri. These plants are also popular with flower arrangers. Propagate by lifting the clumps in spring, dividing them into smaller portions of four to five shoots, and replanting them.

Coriandrum sativum
H 2 ft. S 12 in.
Sun/partial shade
Well-drained
Any Z7

Coriander is a hardy annual originating from the Mediterranean with long-stalked, fernlike, glossy dark green foliage that produces a strong citrus aroma. From midsummer until late autumn, broad, flat clusters of small, cup-shaped white or pale purple flowers about 2 in. across are produced on the tips of shoots. The flowers are followed by pale golden-brown fruits that emit an orangelike scent when dried. Propagate by sowing seeds directly into the soil outdoors in late spring.

Lilium speciosum
H 3–5 ft. S 12 in.
Partial shade
Moist
Acid Z5

This well-known species produces flowers that are so fragrant they are often sold as cut flowers. The rounded bulbs are yellowish to purple-brown in color and produce erect green stems, often with purple markings along their length, and carry evenly scattered, broadly lance-shaped, mid-green leaves. From midsummer through autumn, the large flowers protrude horizontally from the main stem, with the individual blooms having strongly reflexed, wavy-margined petals that are basically white with deeper pink centers. There are some color variants, such as *L. s.* var. *album*, with pure white flowers, and *L. s.* var. *rubrum*, with deep carmine-red flowers. Propagate by lily scaling or by dividing in fall.

PERENNIALS, ANNUALS, & BIENNIALS

Nerine bowdenii
H 30 in. S 3 in.
Sun
Well-drained
Any Z8

Originating from South Africa, this
sturdy, bulbous, hardy, herbaceous
perennial produces clusters of
broad, semierect, strap-shaped,
mid-green leaves that often appear
as the flowers open. In autumn,
open clusters of funnel-shaped,
lilylike, scented pink flowers with
a frilled edge to the petals are
produced above the leaves on
slender green stalks. There is also a
very attractive white-flowered form
of this plant, *Nerine bowdenii* f.
alba. Propagate by sowing seeds
as soon as it is ripe or by dividing
established clumps after they have
finished flowering.

Romneya coulteri
H 4 ft. S 7 ft.
Sun
Well-drained
Alkaline/neutral Z7

This shrubby, herbaceous perennial
originates from California and is
commonly called the Matilija
poppy. It has blue-green, broad
oval leaves that are deeply lobed,
looking almost like large fern
leaves, and that are carried on thick,
blue-green stems. It is grown for its
huge, white poppy flowers, 4–5 in.
across, with a large cluster of
golden stamens and a sweet, exotic
perfume. The flowers appear from
late summer well into fall. Another
species, *R. trichocalyx*, is slightly
smaller and less vigorous than
R. coulteri but produces flowers
that are much more fragrant during
the summer months. Propagate by
taking root cuttings in late winter
or early spring.

Scabiosa atropurpurea
H 3 ft. S 10 in.
Sun
Moderate
Alkaline/neutral Z9

Commonly known as the
pincushion flower or
mourningbride, this is a hardy
biennial with large, solitary,
chrysanthemum-like flowers
ranging from purple to lilac in
color and with a honey scent.
They are borne on long, slender,
pale green, leafless stems from
midsummer into autumn. The
leaves are straplike, with the upper
part divided into narrow segments,
and form a low, matted cluster
reaching no more than 8–12 in.
high. The flowers grow above the
foliage and are excellent as cut
flowers. Propagate by sowing seed
indoors in early spring or outdoors
in late spring.

chapter six

6

Plants for winter

Some of the most fragrant plants flower through the winter months, producing blooms of outstanding scent and beauty. Some of these flowers are delicate in appearance but are capable of withstanding all but the most bitter winter weather conditions. By selecting a range of plants, you can achieve a continuous array of fragrances throughout winter, but be careful not to overdo it. Too many scented plants positioned close together and flowering at the same time will spoil the effect, as the fragrances will overlap one another. Although the beauty of the flowers can be appreciated, each individual fragrance will be lost in a cloud of pleasant but indistinguishable scents.

Winter scent

Each species has its own way of attracting pollinators at this time of year, when the insect population is low. Plants competing for the same pollinators will use different fragrances as attractants. Winter jasmine (*Jasminum nudiflorum*) has honey-scented flowers, *Mahonia japonica* has a fragrance similar to lily of the valley, and *Daphne odora* has a spicy scent. A wider range of fragrances can be found among *Viburnum*, with different species having the scent of cloves, jonquil, heliotrope, or a sweet scent. However, to give the impression that all winter-flowering plants are heavily and pleasantly scented would be wrong. Some have no scent, while others have a pronounced unpleasant smell. For example, the winter-flowering *Helleborus foetidus* is commonly called the stinking hellebore because of its strong aroma, and *Daphne laureola* produces an unpleasant odor.

Tall plants

It is important to strike a balance when positioning winter plants so that you can smell the flowers when they are in bloom, but so you do not have to go to great lengths disguising the spaces they leave when they die back during the summer. Some of the taller growing plants that have a strong perfume can be a good solution to this problem. Plants such as wintersweet (*Chimonanthus praecox*), witch hazel (*Hamamelis*), and *Mahonia* need to be grown farther back in a border because of their size. If they can be grown behind lower-growing deciduous plants so that they are seen in all of their glory through the winter months but are partially obscured during the summer months, then so much the better. However, take all qualities into consideration; *Hamamelis* species also tend to have glorious autumn colors that you will want in full view.

Wall plants

Growing plants close to buildings can be a useful method of gaining the maximum effect from any perfume given off by their flowers, especially when they are positioned close to a window or door that is regularly opened during the flowering period so that even a small amount of the scent can be fully appreciated indoors. Plants grown close to buildings often flower slightly earlier (and for longer) than their counterparts standing farther away in the garden because they benefit from the protection of the walls and their residual heat. Winter-flowering wall plants

Choose your winter plants with care. This Helleborus orientalis *has a mild but attractive scent—unlike the stinking* Helleborus foetidus.

include the yellow-flowered *Jasminum nudiflorum* and the evergreen climber *Clematis cirrhosa balearica*. Unfortunately, the disadvantage to this growth being slightly ahead of the season is that, if a period of cold sets in, these plants are usually casualties and a whole season's flowers and fragrance can be lost overnight.

Bulbs

Bulbs with fragrant flowers look best when planted outdoors in large drifts or groups. This allows the fragrance to make a real impact and is particularly important with small, low-growing bulbs such as *Crocus* and hardy *Cyclamen*. It is easier to let the fragrance rise up to meet you from a large group of flowers than to have to stoop to catch the scent of a few blooms.

Hyacinthus and *Narcissus* bulbs and *Crocus* corms can be "forced" in bowls to bring them into bloom indoors earlier than they would outside (see pages 64–65). These attractive blooms, particularly *Hyacinthus* and some of the *Narcissus*, are valued as much for their heavy perfume as for their color. Forcing these plants to flower ahead of their natural season not only provides interest over the quieter winter period but, with successive plantings, can provide color and fragrance well into the spring.

Indoor fragrance

Fragrance does not have to be confined to the garden, and many scented winter-flowering shrubs can be used as cut flowers, with stems of partly opened flowers brought indoors and placed in water. In the warmth of a room, these flowers will open and gradually envelop the room with a cloud of fragrance, often for a week or more before they need to be replaced.

Winter weather and its effects

The weather is more unreliable in winter than at any other time and can range from heavy, lying snow that smothers the plants, to prolonged rainfall, bitingly cold winds, and frost, depending on where you live. In coastal areas, the conditions will be made less extreme by the influence of the sea and you will rarely get frost, but fog will make the air moist and the winds will be salt-laden. Although deciduous trees and shrubs look dead when they lose their leaves in the winter, the plants have simply withdrawn nutrients back into themselves for protection from the cold weather. They do in fact continue to grow very slowly. Their roots are active throughout (except for a very short period in the middle of winter) and changes take place in the shoots so that, as soon as the weather warms up, the buds will be ready to burst open and the new leaves unfurl or the flowers open.

Jobs for winter

There is no point gardening in winter, is there? Isn't everything dead? It is a season of frosts and cold that is hardly likely to promote outdoor activity. However, this is a misconception because winter is not that different from any other season. It is just that the weather is colder and the growth rate of most plants slows down. Although many of the fragrant plants grown in the garden are resting through the winter months, the gardener is far from inactive, and in many respects, winter in the garden can be as busy as any other season of the year.

Plant care

Check the greenhouse or cold frame constantly for signs of pests or diseases, which take advantage of the protection. Pay attention to hygiene and remove plant debris to cut the risk of infection, particularly if you are reluctant to use chemical controls. Plants that are actively growing in a greenhouse, house, or sunroom need dead flower heads removed, along with any yellowing leaves, before mold starts to grow. Careful water management will ensure that flowering and growth is not impaired by under- or overwatering. Woody indoor plants, such as *Citrus*, tend to produce soft, sappy growth if they are growing in a warm environment with poor winter light levels, and some pruning may be required to keep the growth balanced.

Heavy snowfalls can settle on plants, particularly conifers and evergreens with a larger surface area, and the weight can cause branches to bend or break. Knock the snow off these to help reduce damage, because a torn branch leaves an open wound for infections to enter in spring.

Protection

Save energy by insulating greenhouses and cold frames with bubble wrap or similar insulation. Reducing drafts will save on heat loss and plant casualties. Outdoors, new plants introduced since the previous winter will need protection if the weather turns severe. Wind tends to be the real killer, rather than low temperatures. Evergreens, plants growing in containers, and tall plants, including any over 18 in. that have not been firmly anchored, are the most vulnerable. They can be severely damaged by wind, which can loosen the roots, and need to be refirmed and staked or protected. If your garden is particularly windswept, you may wish to consider planting a windbreak of some sort to reduce the airflow. Creating shelter in the garden will also allow you to better appreciate the fragrance of the plants in the calmer air.

Another problem that the wind causes for these plants is the foliage drying out. Conifers and broad-leaved evergreens suffer windchill damage when freezing winds draw moisture from leaves faster than it can be replaced, resulting in brown, dry foliage on the windward side. When the garden soil is wet or

Small-leaved plants, such as sweet box (Sarcococca hookeriana var. humilis), can cope with snowfall, but remember to shake the snow off plants with a larger surface area in case it causes them to bend and break.

frozen, the roots are unable to take up water to replace the moisture drawn out of the leaves by the wind. A screen of woven plastic mesh or horticultural fleece on the windward side of the plant will reduce the wind's effects and protect the leaves.

During heavy frosts, some plants may benefit from being wrapped in protective fleece, which absorbs at least some of the cold. Plants growing in containers need their roots protected from the cold, either by insulating the container or temporarily moving the whole plant into a more sheltered environment.

Soil preparation

Soil improvement is a winter job because there are areas of bare soil that are only found between plantings. The heavier the soil, the more important it is to dig in early autumn, as winter frost can break down sticky clay soil better than any cultivation tool. For heavy soils, winter frost is an ally rather than an enemy, and the incorporation of compost or other organic matter will benefit both the soil structure and the plants growing in it for years to come.

Construction

Winter is a good time for dealing with construction and landscaping jobs, when sections of the garden may be bare. It is easier to see the garden layout and make changes for the coming spring. If the soil is not too wet to be structurally damaged by foot traffic and wheelbarrows, drainage systems can be installed or improved. Although summer is often regarded as the best time for installing drains in a heavy clay soil, the ground can be rock solid at that time of year, as well as occupied by plants.

Repairs and maintenance

Repairs and maintenance figure prominently during winter, when the lack of vegetation is a bonus. For instance, this is an ideal time to drain and clean pools and ponds and to carry out repairs to pond sides, walls, and liners, while the plants are dormant and the fish lethargic.

The lawn will benefit from attention during late winter and early spring before new growth starts—releveling, changing the shape, increasing the shape and size of borders, and reseeding areas where growth is sparse (or places where the grass has died out altogether). Remember that no work should be carried out if the grass is frozen because footprints made on frozen grass can cause it to turn brown. The reason for this is that the cells within the leaves are full of ice rather than sap in cold weather.

Propagation & planting

Winter can seem like a quiet time in the garden, when nothing is growing and not much is happening. However, there is still plenty of propagating and planting to do. Some seeds need to be chilled during the colder weather in order to germinate later in the year. Species of hardy plants that come true from seeds can be propagated at this time, while named cultivars (which do not come true from seeds) can be grown from cuttings. You may also need to transplant more established plants so that their roots can settle in during the winter, ready to grow in the coming seasons.

Growing from seeds

The seeds of plants such as roses (*Rosa*) need to be exposed to a period of cold—known as stratifying—in order to help them germinate during the following spring and summer. Sowing seeds from this type of plant in late autumn allows it to be chilled to temperatures between 28–35°F during the winter, causing the necessary chemical changes within the seed that will bring about germination later. Other hardy plants, such as *Hamamelis*, can also be propagated from seeds at this time.

Hardwood cuttings

Winter is the ideal time to increase numbers of many of those trees and shrubs that can be propagated by hardwood cuttings. Take sections of the current season's growth and insert them into the garden soil. This method of propagation will produce new large plants within ten to twelve months. If the cuttings are taken before the middle of winter, they will have started to form new roots within a month. Broad-leaved evergreen plants, like *Elaeagnus* and *Mahonia*, can be taken as cuttings and placed under protection in a cold frame to keep them from drying out. Leave the plants in the frame for a whole year so that they have a large enough root system for transplanting.

Division

Many nonwoody plants, such as herbaceous perennials, can be lifted and divided into smaller segments before being replanted. To keep these plants healthy and flowering well, this process should be repeated every three or four years. The most important thing is to discard any old, dead, or diseased parts of the original clump. This will help to reduce pests and diseases on the older plants and keep them from being passed on to the new ones.

Transplanting

It is important to get the maximum benefit from hardy winter-flowering plants, because although many are heavily scented, they may flower for a relatively short time. The period when their fragrance is at its peak is even shorter and usually falls about one-third of the way between the bud's opening and the flower's death. The most obvious approach is to site the plants as close to a path or walkway as possible. Unfortunately, many of the plants that provide glorious winter color have very little worth noting during the rest of the year, so having them at the front of the

Hardy plants such as this Hamamelis x intermedia *'Diane' can be propagated by seeds during the winter months.*

During winter, take cuttings of broad-leaved evergreen plants such as this Mahonia lomariifolia *and place them in a cold frame.*

border means having a potentially dull-looking plant in full view during other seasons. These factors must be kept in mind when making planting decisions.

Bare-root plants

The worst possible time for planting bare-root plants is when the weather is cold and windy. If the roots are subjected to drying winds for as little as twenty minutes, they will be damaged and will need to heal before the plant can start to produce new root growth and establish itself in the new position. If the soil and weather conditions are very bad, the plants can be "heeled in" (temporarily planted in a sheltered part of the garden) and planted into their permanent site when conditions improve.

Container-grown plants

Where the garden soil is wet or heavy (clay), avoid planting container-grown plants until the soil has drained. The reason for this is that many of the loamless composts used for growing plants in containers are very absorbent and will attract water from the surrounding garden soil into the planting hole. This can lead to the plant's roots literally drowning due to lack of oxygen.

Propagating fragrant lilies

You can easily and cheaply increase the number of fragrant plants in your garden (or provide plants for friends and family) by making use of some simple propagation techniques. Lilies, despite looking exotic, are in fact extremely easy to propagate. Using a simple form of leaf cutting, you can produce a large quantity of new plants and enjoy their fragrant, trumpet-shaped flowers the following year.

WHAT YOU NEED

Materials: Lily bulbs, plastic bag, fine-grade sphagnum moss peat or similar compost, labels, fungicide, plant pots

A very simple form of leaf cutting is probably the easiest way to propagate lilies. Removing the outer modified leaves (scales) from the parent bulb can produce large quantities of new plants. This is a highly productive method of increasing plant numbers, as it is possible to remove up to eighty percent of the outer scales from the parent bulb, which will still grow and produce a flower the following year if it is replanted.

This method is usually practiced through the fall and into winter while the bulb is dormant, although the preparation should start earlier in the year. In late summer and early autumn (depending on the species, but definitely after flowering and as the stem begins to turn brown and dry), carefully lift the bulbs from the ground and lay them in a seed tray to dry for two to three days before carefully brushing the soil from the outer scales of the bulb and removing the dead flower stem.

It is particularly important that the bulb is as clean as possible before propagation, as any soil or rotting plant tissue may be a source of infection, which can rapidly spread to healthy lily scales during the warm, humid conditions while the lilies are being propagated.

Tip: Some lilies can be propagated by small, pea-sized bulblets, which form in the angle where the leaf and stem join together.

Remove the outer scales from the parent bulb by breaking them off at the point where they are attached to the basal plate of the bulb. It is important to work systematically around the bulb to avoid damaging any scales unnecessarily.

Place the scales in a plastic bag and add enough peat (or compost) so the bag contains equal amounts of peat and scales. Add the fungicide, close the bag, and turn the contents over several times so that the peat, scales, and fungicide are evenly mixed.

Loosely tie up the bag and label it with the plant's name and the date. Place the bag in a warm, dark place (like a closet) for two to three months. Each scale should now have at least one small embryo bulb (bulblet) about ¼ in. long, with white fibrous roots.

Each scale, complete with bulblets, can be potted into a small 3-in. pot with just the tip of the old scale showing, and placed outdoors.

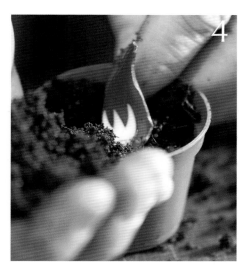

As the weather becomes warmer in the spring, new grasslike leaves will appear through the compost, growing from the bulblets.

In the fall, these young bulbs can be planted in the garden soil and may flower the following year.

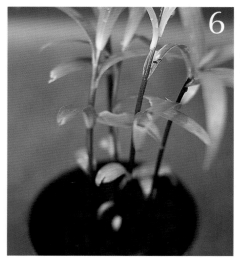

Taking root cuttings

Propagating plants from root cuttings can be a simple and quick way of increasing plant numbers, but it remains one of the least-known propagation techniques. It is the standard method of propagating a few plant species, mainly herbaceous perennials and alpines, but a large number of fragrant trees, shrubs, and climbers can also be grown in this way.

WHAT YOU NEED
Tools: Garden fork, pruning shears, sharp knife
Materials: Plants such as *Acanthus spinosus*, *Wisteria*, *Phlox*, *Romneya*, *Chaenomeles*, *Sassafras*, and *Aesculus parviflora*; plant pots; compost; grit

The beauty of propagating plants from root cuttings is that a large number of plants can be produced from a small number of roots without disfiguring the plant, which can sometimes happen with stem cuttings. The plants that can be propagated from this type of cutting have roots containing dormant buds, which have the capacity to produce new shoots and stems. Each new plant should look identical to the parent it was taken from.

Root cuttings fall into two basic categories: cuttings from plants with thick, fleshy roots (such as *Romneya*, *Aesculus*, and *Echinops*) that can be inserted vertically into propagating compost; and cuttings from plants with thin, wiry roots (such as *Phlox*, *Eryngium*, and *Hesperis*) that are laid horizontally on top of the propagating compost. The best time to propagate plants from root cuttings is when the plant is fully dormant. This is usually in late winter and early spring. Although it is possible to take this type of cutting at other times during the plant's life cycle, the rate of success is usually much poorer.

> **Tip:** Root cuttings can be used as a method of combating some plant pests. Some species of *Phlox*, for example, are propagated from root cuttings in an attempt to combat eelworms, which live only in the leaves and stems.

Using a garden fork, carefully dig around the roots of the plant that is to be propagated so that some roots are exposed and clearly visible.

Using a pair of pruning shears, cut through some of the strongest and healthiest roots and remove them. Replace the soil around the plant and gently firm it back into position.

Wash the roots carefully to remove as much soil as possible. This will make it easier to see where to cut and reduces excessive wear and tear on knives and shears.

Using a sharp knife, cut the roots into 2-in.-long sections with a flat cut (at a right angle to the root) at the top of the cutting, and a slanting cut at the bottom. This ensures that the cuttings are not inserted into the compost upside down.

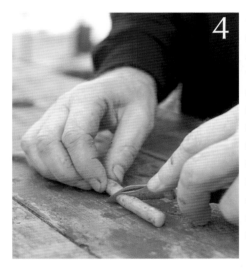

If the cuttings are thick and fleshy, gently push them into a pot of compost so that the top of each cutting is level with the surface of the compost. If the cuttings are thin, lay them horizontally over the surface of the compost.

Cover the cuttings with a layer of grit. This will allow air to reach the top of the cuttings without letting them dry out. It also acts as an effective barrier against slugs.

Preparing to plant

The first step to successful planting is, of course, to select the plant carefully. Look for a well-balanced, healthy plant with evenly spaced branches and a strong structure. There should be no sign of damaged or broken branches or any visible sign of pests and diseases. Trees and shrubs should have a wide-angled joint between the branch and stem for the main structural or framework branches. Reject any plants with excess weeds in the compost. How and when you plant will then depend on whether your fragrant plant is a container-grown, bare-root, or rootballed plant.

Container-grown

Plants grown in containers can be purchased and planted at any time of year, provided the soil and weather conditions are suitable for the species. For this reason, container-grown plants are a convenient way of adding new plants to the garden. Remove the container and examine the root system of the plant, discarding any with damaged roots or excess sucker growths.

Bare-root

These are plants where all of the soil has been removed from around the roots. The roots are usually wrapped in plastic to protect them from frost or drying out. Bare-root plants are only available when the plants are dormant, ready to be planted whenever the soil and weather conditions are suitable. They tend to be cheaper than container-grown or rootballed plants.

Rootballed

Rootballed plants have soil around the roots and are tightly wrapped in burlap. They are usually available between autumn and spring and can be planted whenever conditions are suitable.

OPPOSITE *The key to successful planting is to choose plants with a well-balanced structure, such as gracefully arching* Abeliophyllum distichum.

Choose a well-balanced plant with evenly spaced branches and no damaged foliage or broken branches or stems. Remove the root wrapping and examine the root system of the plant, discarding any with rotting or damaged roots.

Staking and supporting

Newly planted trees can support themselves once the roots have anchored but will require support initially, especially in exposed positions. For bare-root trees, position the stake into the planting hole before planting. This will ensure that the tree support is firmly fixed into the soil and the roots are not damaged by knocking in the stake after planting. Even on exposed sites, the tree only needs anchoring near the base with a tie 6–8 in. above soil level. Provided the roots are static, they can establish quickly, leaving the stem to flex in the wind and thicken naturally. Position the stake on the windward side of the tree so that it tugs at the stake rather than blowing against it, which could cause bruising or breakage. For container-grown or rootballed trees, drive the stake into the surrounding soil at about a forty-five-degree angle to avoid damaging the plant's root system. The top of the stake should point toward the direction of the prevailing wind to ensure that the stem drives the stake farther into the ground as the wind blows it. Tie the tree to the support about 1 ft. above ground level.

SELECTING YOUR FRAGRANT PLANT

TYPE OF PLANT	ADVANTAGES	DISADVANTAGES
Container-grown plants	• Available year-round • Ideal for plants that resent root disturbance or suffer reduced growth after being transplanted	• More expensive, often by as much as 30–40 percent • Often difficult to support or stake • Larger specimens can be very heavy and awkward to handle due to the volume of compost in the container
Bare-root plants	• Plants are relatively light due to lack of compost or soil around the roots • Often much easier to support or stake while planting because the roots are visible • Usually less expensive than container-grown plants	• Only available for about six months of the year (when the plant is dormant)
Rootballed plants	• Usually less expensive than container-grown plants • Better for plants such as conifers and broad-leaved evergreens that resent having their roots dry	• Often difficult to support or stake • Only available for about six months of the year (when the plant is dormant) • Larger specimens can be very heavy and awkward to handle due to the volume of compost in the container

Protecting climbers & wall shrubs

Many fragrant climbers and wall shrubs are only marginally hardy and actually need a wall or fence for protection and warmth, as well as for support. During cold winter periods, however, additional protection may be needed to ensure that these plants make it through the winter unharmed and produce flowers, fruit, and fragrance the following year.

WHAT YOU NEED

Tools: Pruning shears, screwdriver, scissors, staple gun
Materials: Garden twine or twist ties, L-brackets or cup hooks, screws, garden fleece, long bamboo canes

In spring, summer, and fall, the residual heat provided by supporting walls or fences can often be sufficient to help fragrant climbers and wall shrubs thrive rather than struggle, making the difference as to whether a plant can flower and produce fruit. During the cold winter months, however, climbers such as the passionflower (*Passiflora*), shrubs such as Spanish broom (*Spartium junceum*), and fan-trained trees such as myrtle (*Luma*) and *Ceanothus* may all need additional protection.

A fixed but adjustable cover offers the best option, so that it can be raised on warm days and lowered for cold spells. Any insulation material used should allow some light to reach the plant, and allow some airflow so that the plant does not suffer from fungal rots.

Should the weather turn warm, the protection can be rolled up to allow the sun to warm the plant. This will help to keep the plant from starting to grow too early in the year. It will also prevent the existing growth from becoming too soft and will discourage any harmful pests and diseases from harboring under the shelter.

> **Tip:** Growing some of the more tender climbers, such as passionflowers (*Passiflora*), through evergreen shrubs will also provide them with some winter protection.

Trim the plant to remove any damaged growth and tie in any loose or rubbing shoots. Fix four brackets or hooks into the fence or wall—two just above the climber and two near the base of the plant. Both pairs should be about 6 ft. apart.

Cut a length of garden fleece 6 ft. wide and long enough to cover the full height of the plant; allow an extra 4 in. at the top and the bottom. Fold over these 4-in. ends and staple them in position.

Thread a 7-ft. cane through the fold at the top the fleece.

Thread another 7-ft. cane through the fold at the bottom of the fleece.

Hang one cane between the top pair of brackets or over the top hooks, and fix in place.

Allow the fleece to drape down in front of the plant before fixing the bottom cane into the lower pair of brackets or under the bottom hooks.

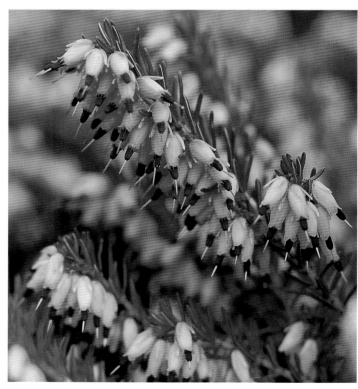

TREES

KEY INFORMATION

H: The average height the plant can reach

S: The average spread the plant can achieve

Sun/partial shade/shade:
The position the plant prefers

Well-drained/moderate/moist:
How much water the plant needs

Acid/alkaline/neutral/any:
The plant's preferred soil type

Z1 to Z10: The minimum winter temperature (zone) the plant can withstand

Zone 1: below –50°F
Zone 2: –50 to –40°F
Zone 3: –40 to –30°F
Zone 4: –30 to –20°F
Zone 5: –20 to –10°F
Zone 6: –10 to 0°F
Zone 7: 0 to 10°F
Zone 8: 10 to 20°F
Zone 9: 20 to 30°F
Zone 10: 30 to 40°F

Amomyrtus luma
H 23 ft. S 13 ft.
Sun
Well-drained
Any Z9

This multistemmed tree has an upright habit and beautiful smooth bark that becomes loose and scaly with age. The lance-shaped aromatic leaves are a coppery bronze color when young, changing to a glossy dark green with age. They are about 1 in. long and arranged in opposite pairs along orange-brown stems. From late winter onward, sweetly scented, creamy white flowers are borne in clusters of up to ten on the branches. The flowers are often followed by aromatic, edible, reddish-black fruit later in the year. Propagate by sowing seeds in a cold frame during spring or by taking semiripe cuttings in late summer.

Azara microphylla
H 32 ft. S 13 ft.
Sun
Well-drained/moderate
Any Z7

Originating from Chile and Argentina, this is an evergreen tree or large shrub with slender, arching branches and oval-shaped, glossy dark green leaves with a finely toothed margin, often paler on the underside. In late winter and into spring, dense clusters of greenish-yellow, vanilla-scented flowers up to ½ in. across are produced. Prune immediately after flowering by cutting the flower-bearing shoots back to four or five buds. This is the hardiest azara and is a perfect choice for growing against a hot, sunny wall or as a tree in a sheltered garden. Propagate by taking semiripe cuttings from the new side shoots in mid- to late summer.

Cornus mas
H 16 ft. S 16 ft.
Sun
Well-drained
Any Z5

The cornelian cherry is a small,
hardy tree that produces fragrant
yellow blossoms in the depths of
winter and well into spring. The
small flowers form tight, golden
yellow clusters held close to
the naked, twiggy branches. By
midspring, glossy, broadly oval-
shaped, mid-green leaves are
produced in opposite pairs along
the branches after the flowers have
faded. There are several different
cultivars of this plant that are less
vigorous and provide additional
interest at other times of the year,
such as *C. m.* 'Aurea' and *C. m.*
'Variegata.' Propagate by sowing
seeds outdoors in autumn.

Eucalyptus perriniana
H 32 ft. S 16 ft.
Sun
Well-drained
Acid/neutral Z8

Eucalyptus are interesting evergreen
trees grown mainly for their
aromatic, blue-gray, leathery leaves
and peeling stems. The leaf shape
varies with the age of the plant—the
juvenile leaves are almost circular,
but as the plant matures, the new
leaves are straplike and a blue-
green color. In the early years, the
stem is blue-gray, but as the tree
ages, the old outer bark peels away
and hangs in long strips before
falling off. Some species, such
as *E. pulverulenta*, produce clusters
of up to three white flowers in
winter. Propagate by sowing seeds
in spring.

Prunus mume
H 29 ft. S 29 ft.
Sun
Well-drained
Any Z6

This deciduous tree is known as
the Japanese apricot, although it
originates from China and Korea.
It has a spreading habit, and the
rounded, tapered leaves are up
to 4 in. long, dark green in color,
and held on arching green shoots.
In late winter and early spring,
before the leaves emerge, sweetly
fragrant, cup-shaped flowers up to
1 in. across are carried in pairs
along the branches. Flower color
varies from pure white through to
dark pink. Later, rounded, yellow,
hairy, apricotlike, edible fruits are
produced. Propagate by taking
softwood cuttings in summer or
sowing seeds in autumn.

SHRUBS

Coronilla valentina subsp. glauca
H 3 ft. S 3 ft.
Sun
Well-drained
Any Z9

This shrub originates from
Southeastern Europe and has a
dense, bushy habit with slender,
twiggy growth and bluish-green
leaves up to 2 in. long. These
evergreen leaves are divided into
segments, often as many as nine in
all. Clusters of up to fourteen bright
yellow, sweetly scented, pealike
flowers are produced in late winter
and early spring and again in late
summer, and often are followed by
slender pods up to 2 in. long. There
are a number of forms of this plant,
including C. v. subsp. glauca
'Citrina' (pale yellow flowers) and
C. v. subsp. glauca 'Variegata'
(creamy white margin to the leaves).
Propagate by sowing seeds in a
cold frame as soon as it is ripe
or by taking semiripe cuttings in
late summer.

Daphne sericea
H 20 in. S 20 in.
Sun
Moderate
Acid/neutral Z8

This slow-growing evergreen shrub
benefits from some shelter from cold
winds and grows with a compact,
rounded habit and glossy dark green
leaves with a downy underside. It
produces a spectacular display of
intensely fragrant, clove-scented
flowers in late winter and early
spring. These are pinkish-purple
with white markings, carried in
clusters of up to fifteen blooms. On
a warm, calm day, the scent carries
for a great distance around the
plant. Prune only to remove dead
or damaged wood and move as
little as possible because it resents
disturbance. Propagate by taking
semiripe cuttings in summer.

Erica x darleyensis
H 12 in. S 2 ft.
Sun
Well-drained/moderate
Acid Z6

A hybrid between E. carnea and
E. erigena, the winter heath forms a
dense, bushy evergreen shrub with
small, narrow, lance-shaped leaves
that are slightly grooved and mid-
green in color. White to rose-pink
urn-shaped flowers up to ¼ in. long
are carried in spikes up to 4 in. long
from late winter and into early
spring. The cultivar E. x darleyensis
'Furzey' produces masses of honey-
scented flowers. This plant must
have acidic soil. Propagate by taking
semiripe cuttings from the new
shoots in mid- to late summer and
placing them in a cold frame, or by
mound-layering in spring.

Erica x veitchii
H 7 ft. S 30 in.
Sun
Well-drained/moderate
Neutral Z8

The hybrid tree heath is a
hybrid between *E. arborea* and
E. lusitanica. It forms an erect, open
shrub with small, narrow, mid-green
evergreen leaves. From late winter
into spring, it produces ¼-in.-long
white, urn-shaped flowers in spikes
up to 12 in. long. The cultivar
E. x *veitchii* 'Exeter' produces a
strong display of scented flowers.
This plant is unusual among
heathers in that it will tolerate some
lime in the soil, although it prefers
acidic soil. Propagate by taking
semiripe cuttings from the new
shoots in mid- to late summer and
placing them in a cold frame.

Eupatorium sordidum
H 10 ft. S 8 ft.
Sun/partial shade
Moist
Alkaline Z10

A native of Mexico, this is a large,
bushy, rounded shrub, with young
stems that have a covering of
reddish, woolly hairs. The deep-
green leaves are arranged in
opposite pairs and are broadly
spear-shaped and approximately
4 in. long. They have a finely
toothed margin, pointed tip, and a
red, feltlike coating on the lower
surface. From late autumn into
winter, the tips of the tall stems bear
violet flowers in broad, rounded
clusters up to 5 in. across, with a
strong resinous fragrance. Propagate
by sowing seeds or taking softwood
tip cuttings in spring.

Hamamelis x intermedia
H 10 ft. S 13 ft.
Sun/partial shade
Moderate
Acid/neutral Z5

The witch hazels are very distinctive
and beautiful deciduous shrubs that
produce attractive winter flower
displays on their bare branches.
The sweetly fragrant flowers have
a twisted, spidery appearance, with
small, feathery, slightly curled petals
that are mainly colored in various
shades of yellow, although some
cultivars have darker flowers in
shades of coppery red. The large
leaves are mid-green in color,
broadly oval, and provide a
stunning display in autumn, when
they turn shades of yellow, orange,
scarlet, and red before falling from
the branches. Propagate by taking
softwood cuttings in late summer
or by grafting onto a rootstock
in midwinter.

SHRUBS

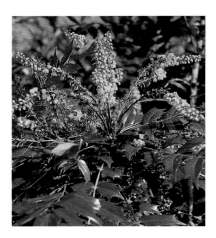

Lonicera x _purpusii_
H 7 ft. S 8 ft.
Sun/shade
Moderate
Any Z6

This winter-flowering shrubby honeysuckle is grown for its fragrant flowers, which are arranged in pairs and are usually carried on the bare branches in small clusters. The flowers are basically tubular in shape, opening out to a broad mouth, and are usually white in color with pale yellow to golden markings. The deciduous to semievergreen leaves are broadly oval in shape and mid- to deep green in color. They are carried in pairs on thin, twiggy, reddish-purple stems, gradually developing an open, spreading habit. Propagate by taking hardwood cuttings of nonflowering shoots in winter or softwood cuttings in midsummer.

Mahonia lomarifolia
H 10 ft. S 7 ft.
Partial shade
Well-drained
Any Z7

Originating from western China, this tough, hardy shrub has an upright habit and glossy, dark green, leathery evergreen leaves up to 2 ft. long and subdivided to make up a compound leaf of many lance-shaped, sharply toothed leaflets. From late autumn until midwinter, it produces flowers with a strong, distinctive fragrance. They are a rich yellow and are carried on the shoot tips in dense, upright spikes up to 8 in. long. The flowers are often followed by black, oval-shaped berries in summer. Propagate by taking semiripe cuttings in late summer or early autumn and placing them in a cold frame.

Mahonia x _media_
H 13 ft. S 10 ft.
Partial shade
Well-drained
Any Z7

A hybrid of _M. japonica_ and _M. lomarifolia_, this hardy shrub has an upright habit and glossy evergreen leaves composed of many lance-shaped leaflets. From late autumn until early spring, it produces dense spikes of yellow flowers, up to 16 in. long, that have a strong lily of the valley fragrance. A cultivar worth considering for a smaller garden is _M._ x _m._ 'Winter Sun,' which has arching spikes of bright yellow flowers. Propagate by taking semiripe cuttings in late summer or early autumn and placing them in a cold frame.

Sarcococca hookeriana
H 5 ft. S 7 ft.
Shade
Moderate
Any Z6

This hardy evergreen shrub,
commonly known as the Christmas
box, has a suckering habit and often
forms a dense thicket of growth. The
tough, leathery leaves are broadly
lance-shaped and a mid- to dark
green color, carried on sturdy, erect
green stems. In winter, clusters of
white, sweetly fragrant flowers are
produced in the leaf joints, to be
followed by purple-black fruit later
in the year. *Sarcococca hookeriana*
var. *digyna* has narrower leaves.
Propagate by sowing seeds in a cold
frame as soon as it is ripe, by taking
semiripe cuttings in late summer, or
by removing suckers from the plants
soon after flowering.

Skimmia japonica
H 10 ft. S 16 ft.
Sun
Moderate
Any Z7

The Japanese skimmias are slow-
growing, hardy evergreens with
thick, leathery, broadly oval-shaped
leaves that are aromatic when
crushed and carried on stocky,
reddish-green stems. The male and
female flowers are often reddish-
pink in bud before developing as
spikes of white, sweetly scented
blooms on separate plants from late
winter well into spring. These are
followed by orange-red berries on
the female plants, which persist
throughout the following autumn
and winter. Skimmias are ideal
for city gardening because they are
tolerant to atmospheric pollution.
Propagate by taking semiripe
cuttings in late summer and placing
them in a cold frame.

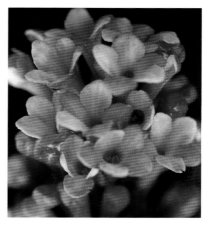

Viburnum x bodnantense 'Dawn'
H 7 ft. S 5 ft.
Sun/partial shade
Moderate
Any Z7

A spectacular upright shrub for
winter color, this plant will produce
its clusters of rich pink flowers on
bare stems continuously from late
autumn until early spring, although
it will pause in periods of severe
weather. On a warm, calm day,
the sweet fragrance will carry
some distance from the plant. As
the flowers fade, the coarse-looking
leaves begin to emerge, bronze-
green at first, aging to dark green.
It is ideal for the back of a border
but should be accessible so that the
fragrance can be appreciated. Prune
only to maintain the health of the
plant. Propagate by taking soft-tip
cuttings in summer.

CLIMBERS & WALL SHRUBS

Abeliophyllum distichum
H 5 ft. S 5 ft.
Sun
Well-drained
Any Z5

A native of Korea, this attractive
shrub has an open, spreading habit
and makes an excellent wall shrub
with thin, light brown, arching
shoots. This plant can reach over
8 ft. when grown against a wall. The
oval-shaped deciduous leaves are
arranged in opposite pairs. They are
about 3 in. long and a dull matte-
green color, often turning a reddish-
purple in autumn. In late winter and
early spring, small, sweetly fragrant,
cross-shaped white flowers with
pink markings are produced in long,
slender clusters in the leaf joints.
Propagate by layering or taking
semiripe cuttings in summer.

Chimonanthus praecox
H 13 ft. S 10 ft.
Sun
Well-drained
Any Z7

The wintersweet is a large shrub
ideal for training against a wall or
fence. It has tough, waxy flowers
that have narrow petals colored pale
translucent yellow with a purple
center, opening from midwinter
onward. The blooms have a
delicate, spicy fragrance. Although
hardy, this large, upright shrub is
slow to establish and may take
several years before flowers are
produced. The lance-shaped, glossy
mid-green, deciduous leaves are up
to 8 in. long and are produced after
flowering has finished. Propagate
by sowing seeds in a cold frame
as soon as it is ripe or by taking
softwood cuttings in summer.

Edgeworthia chrysantha
H 5 ft. S 5 ft.
Sun/partial shade
Moderate
Any Z8

Commonly known as the yellow
paperbush, this deciduous shrub
has an open habit and lax branches,
gradually forming a dome-shaped
bush. The oval-shaped, dark green
leaves are up to 6 in. long and are
usually clustered close to the branch
tips. In late winter and early spring,
dense clusters of small, yellow,
tubular flowers around 2 in. across
are produced, each flower with a
strong fragrance of cloves. This plant
may need protection, and for this
reason, it is better trained against
a wall. Propagate by sowing seeds
in containers in a cold frame in
autumn or by taking semiripe
cuttings in summer.

CLIMBERS & WALL SHRUBS

Jasminum nudiflorum
H 10 ft. S 10 ft.
Sun
Moderate
Any Z6

Commonly known as the winter
jasmine, this popular deciduous
plant is outstanding in winter,
especially when grown as a wall
shrub. The thin, whippy, almost
leafless stems are square in shape
and green in color, which gives
the whole plant an evergreen
appearance. It is much valued for its
small, sweetly fragrant, tubular, star-
shaped yellow flowers, which open
from late autumn through early
spring. The variegated form of this
plant, *J. n.* 'Aureum,' has golden
yellow splashes on the leaves. This
plant can be grown in almost any
situation and almost any soil.
Propagate in autumn by taking
semiripe cuttings or tip layers,
which occur naturally wherever
the stems touch the soil.

Lonicera fragrantissima
H 7 ft. S 10 ft.
Sun/shade
Moderate
Any Z5

This is a very attractive deciduous
shrub and produces one of the
most fragrant winter displays on its
naked branches. The plant produces
frequent flushes of honey-scented,
creamy white flowers from late
autumn to early spring. The
deciduous to semievergreen leaves
are broadly oval-shaped and are
carried in pairs on thin, twiggy
stems with attractive light brown
bark. The leaves are deep green on
the upper surface and bluish-green
beneath. This shrub is often grown
against a wall to keep its spreading
habit and arching branches under
control. Propagate by taking
hardwood cuttings of nonflowering
shoots in winter or softwood
cuttings in midsummer.

Viburnum tinus
H 10 ft. S 10 ft.
Sun/partial shade
Moderate
Any Z7

This hardy evergreen shrub is
commonly called the laurustinus.
It has upright growth when young
but develops a rather open, round-
topped and spreading habit as it
ages. The smooth, broadly oval,
dark green leaves have paler green
undersides and are arranged in pairs
along the dark greenish-brown
stems, with each stem ending in a
flat cluster of small, lightly clove-
scented, tubular white flowers,
which last throughout the winter
months. Possibly the best plant is
V. t. 'Eve Price,' which has flowers
of a deep rose-pink in bud,
opening to white flushed with
pink. Propagate by taking semiripe
cuttings in early summer.

HERBACEOUS PLANTS & BULBS

Crocus chrysanthus Group
H 2 in. S 1 in.
Sun/partial shade
Well-drained
Any Z4

This large group of hardy crocus
hybrids related to _C. chrysanthus_
flower in late winter and early
spring. They have short, dull gray to
mid-green leaves, and each plant
can produce up to four sweetly
scented flowers. There is a vast
range of flower colors, ranging from
white and cream through to pale
and golden yellow, orange, and
deeper shades such as blues,
mauves, and purples. These plants
are suitable for forcing indoors,
and, after flowering, they can be
planted out to naturalize in the
garden. Propagate by dividing
when the plant is dormant after
the leaves have died down.

Cyclamen coum
H 3 in. S 4 in.
Shade
Well-drained
Any Z6

This hardy cyclamen is an incredibly
tough little tuberous perennial plant,
with almost round or broadly oval-
shaped dark green leaves with
pronounced silver or gray markings
held above the ground on curling
red stems. _C. coum_ produces
delicately scented flowers varying
from pure white to shades of pink
to carmine red in the depths of
winter, often all growing tightly
grouped together in the same
group or colony. There is a form
with white flowers and dark purple-
red markings named _C. coum_ f.
albissimum. Propagate by sowing
seeds as soon as it is ripe.

Cymbidium
H 2 ft. S 3 ft.
Partial shade
Well-drained
Any Z9

Originating from tropical southeast
Asia and Australia, these versatile
plants have become popular
houseplants in recent years. The
best cymbidium orchids for use in
the home are the modern cultivars
with small pseudobulbs. They have
long, arching, straplike leaves up
to 16 in. long, usually mid- to light
green in color, with long, slender
stems bearing as many as thirty
flowers up to 3 in. across in a single
season. The blooms can vary in
color from blackish-red through
shades of pink, yellow, white, and
even green, and they are often
fragrant. Propagate by dividing
after flowering.

HERBACEOUS PLANTS & BULBS

Eranthis
H 3 in. S 2 in.
Sun/shade
Well-drained
Any Z5

The winter aconite (*E. hyemalis*) is
much valued for its early flowering.
In late winter and early spring,
small, yellow, buttercup-like flowers
appear, with a green frill of leaves,
held above the ground on a green
stem. The flowers have a light,
sweet fragrance. *E.* x *tubergenii*
is a slightly earlier flowering hybrid
of *E. cilicica* and *E. hyemalis*, and
E. x *t.* 'Guinea Gold' produces
deeper golden yellow flowers with
a deliciously sweet fragrance.
Treated as a bulb, it is actually
a tuberous hardy perennial with
attractive pale green, deeply cut
leaves. Propagate by dividing when
the plant is dormant after the leaves
have died down.

Galanthus nivalis
H 4 in. S 4 in.
Partial shade
Well-drained
Any Z4

The common snowdrop is a very
hardy winter-flowering bulb that has
a clump-forming habit. It is grown
for its pretty white, honey-scented
blooms. The pendulous flowers are
produced from midwinter onward,
carried singly on slender green
stalks. The flat, strap-shaped leaves
are a dull mid-green with a slightly
bluish sheen to them, arranged in
pairs, usually one on either side of
the flower stalk. Several cultivars
have started to become popular.
G. n. 'Flore-plena' has double white
flowers and *G. n.* 'Samuel Arnott'
produces larger flowers up to 1½ in.
in length. Propagate by lifting and
dividing clumps immediately after
flowering has finished.

Narcissus papyraceus
H 16 in. S 2–6 in.
Sun
Moderate
Any Z8

This plant is often called the paper
white narcissus and is even sold as
N. 'Paper White.' It has long, broad,
mid-green leaves, held very erect
above ground level; in the center
of each group of leaves is a round,
mid-green flower stem that carries
up to ten clear white flowers that
are very fragrant. Although this is
a winter-flowering plant, it is not
as hardy as some species and will
benefit from shelter, so ensure that
a small amount of frost protection
is provided. Lift and divide every
three to five years, six weeks after
flowering.

GLOSSARY & INDEX GLOSSARY & INDEX... GLOSSARY & INDEX GLOSSARY & INDEX GLOSSARY & INDEX

GLOSSARY

Acclimatization (acclimation)
Adjusting plants to different conditions (usually cooler) than those in which they are growing

Aerate (soil)
Loosen by physical or mechanical means to allow the penetration of air; for example, using a tined fork to aerate the lawn

Alkaline
A substance (soil) with a pH value of 7 or higher

Alpine
A plant that originates from mountainous regions; often applied to rock garden plants

Alternate (buds/leaves)
Leaves that occur at different levels on opposite sides of the stem

Aminoides
A chemical found in some white or off-white flowers that makes them smell of ammonia

Annual
A plant that completes its reproduction cycle in one year

Anther
The pollen-bearing tip of the flower's stamen (male floral parts)

Apex
The tip of a shoot or branch

Apical bud
The uppermost bud in the growing point of a stem (also known as the *terminal bud*)

Aquatic
Any plant that grows in water (may be anchored or free-floating)

Aromatic
Spicy fragrance usually emitted from leaves

Axil
The angle at the point where the leaf or branch joins the main stem of a plant

Axillary bud
A bud that occurs in the leaf axil

Backfill
The operation of refilling a trench or hole in the ground

Bare-root
Plants that are offered for sale with no soil on their roots (usually grown in a field and dug up for sale)

Bark
A protective layer of cells that occurs on the outer surface of the plant's roots and stems of woody plants

Basal
A shoot or bud arising from the base of a plant

Basal plate
The compressed stem of a bulb

Base dressing
Fertilizer or organic matter incorporated into the soil before planting or sowing

Bedding plants
Plants arranged in mass groupings (beds) to form a colorful temporary display

Biennial
A plant that completes its growing cycle in two growing seasons—germinates and produces roots and leaves in its first year, flowers and produces seeds before dying in the second year; for example, foxglove

Blanch
a) To exclude light from sections of a plant in order to keep the tissues soft and supple
b) To plunge sections of a plant in hot water in order to keep the tissues soft and supple

Bleeding
The excessive flow of sap from spring-pruned plants

Blind bud
A bud that fails to produce a terminal bud

Bog plant
A plant that prefers to grow in damp soil (also known as a *marginal*)

Bract
A modified leaf often brightly colored to appear flowerlike; for example, clematis

Branch
A shoot growing directly from the main stem of a woody plant

Break
A shoot growing from a bud as a result of pruning

Broadcasting
The technique of spreading fertilizer or seeds randomly

Bud
A condensed shoot containing an embryonic shoot or flower

Bud union
The point where a cultivar is budded onto a rootstock

Budding
A propagation technique joining two (or more) plants together

Bulb
A storage organ consisting of thick, fleshy leaves arranged on a compressed stem (see *basal plate*) found below soil level

Bush
A multibranched plant with a number of branches of similar size

Calcicole
A plant that prefers a soil that is alkaline (pH 7+), usually a limey soil

Calcifuge
A plant that prefers a soil that is acidic (pH 7-), usually a peaty or organic soil

Callus
The plant tissue that forms as a protective cover over a cut or wounded surface

Calyx
The outer green ring or whorl of a flower, made up of a number of sepals enclosing the petals

Capillary watering
Where plants draw up water into a container from a saturated base

Chilling
A period of low temperature (usually 36°F) required by plants during dormancy to stimulate flower development

Chipping
Cutting bulbs into small sections to propagate them

Chlorophyll
The green plant pigment that is mainly responsible for light absorption and photosynthesis in plants

Climber
A self-supporting plant capable of growing vertically

Cloche
A small, clear, portable structure used for protecting plants

Clone
A collective term for a number of plants that have been propagated from a single individual

Cold frame
A low, clear, portable or permanent structure used for protecting plants from the elements

Companion planting
Growing certain plant combinations close together to overcome pest and disease problems organically

Compound leaf
A leaf consisting of a number of small segments (leaflets)

Compost
a) Potting media made to a standard formula; loam- or peat-based
b) Well-rotted organic matter such as garden waste

Conifer
A classification of plants that have naked ovules often borne in cones, and narrow, needlelike foliage

Corm
An underground modified stem forming a storage organ

Cotyledon
The seed leaves (first leaves) on a seedling; can be:
a) Dicotyledon—plants with two seed leaves
b) Monocotyledon—plants with one seed leaf

Crown
The growing point of an herbaceous perennial originating at soil level

Cultivar
A plant form that originated in cultivation rather than having been found growing in the wild

Cutting
A portion of a plant that is used for propagation

Deadheading
The deliberate removal of dead flower heads or seed-bearing fruits

Deciduous
Plants that produce new leaves in the spring and shed them in the fall

Dieback
The death of plant growth downward from the shoot tip

Disbudding
The removal of unwanted buds to produce fewer, but much larger, flowers

Distillation
The process of heating liquids to get the different components to separate, usually as vapor

Division
A method of propagation that is used to increase the number of plants by splitting them up into smaller units

Dormancy
A period of reduced growth through the winter

Drainage
The free movement of surplus water through the soil/compost

Drill
A narrow, straight line into which seeds are sown

Dry storage
A method of storing edible plants in readiness for use

Earthing up
Mounding up the soil around the base of a plant

Edging shears
Long-handled shears used for trimming lawn edges from a standing position

Enfleurage
The extraction of perfumes from flowers using fats

Epicormic shoots
Shoots that develop from dormant adventitious buds on the main stem of a plant (often referred to as "water shoots")

Ericaceous
A member of the Erica family, which likes acidic soil conditions (see *calcifuge*)

Essential oil
A volatile oil that gives plants their characteristic smell and that is usually produced and stored in the petals or sepals of flowers, but is also found in leaves, bark, and roots

Evergreen
Plants that retain their actively growing leaves through the winter

Fertile
A soil that is rich in nutrients and biological life

Fertilizer
An organic or inorganic compound used to supply nutrition to plants to help them grow

Fibrous roots
Fine, multibranched roots of a plant

Flat
A low-sided box or tray used for propagating young plants or seeds

Fleece
Light, woven material used to protect plants from frost or as a barrier against insect pests

Floating mulch
A sheet of plastic or woven material used for protecting plants from frost, this type of mulch stretches with the plants as they grow

Flower
The part of a plant (often highly colored) that contains the reproductive organs

Force
To induce plants to start growing earlier than they would naturally

Fork
A tined digging implement used for cultivating soil

Formative pruning
A pruning method carried out on young plants to establish a desired plant shape and branch structure

Fragrance
Sweet scent or pleasant smell

Framework
The main permanent branch structure of a woody plant

Frost pocket
A location where cold air accumulates

Fruit
The seed-bearing vessel on a plant

Fruit set
The successful formation of fruits

Fungicide
A chemical used to control fungal disease

Germination
The physical and chemical process by which a seed develops into a plant

Glycoside
A derivative formed from a simple sugar and another molecule by the elimination of water

Graft union
The point where a cultivar is grafted onto a rootstock

Grafting
A propagation method involving the artificial joining of two or more separate plants together

Greenhouse
A glass- or plastic-clad structure used to grow plants under controlled (protected) conditions

Ground cover
The term used to describe low-growing plants

Gum
Any viscous matter exuded by a plant that hardens on contact with the air

Half hardy
A plant that can tolerate low temperatures but is killed by frost

Hardening off
Adjusting plants to different conditions (usually cooler) than those in which they are growing

Hardy
A plant that can tolerate temperatures below freezing without protection

Harvesting
The gathering or collecting of plant produce for storage or consumption

GLOSSARY

Herbaceous
A nonwoody plant with an annual top and a perennial root system or storage organ

Herbicide
A chemical used to kill weeds

Hoeing
A method of shallow cultivation used to kill weed seedlings

Houseplants
Tender plants grown indoors for decoration

Humus
The organic residue of decayed organic material

Hybrid
A plant derived from crossing two other genetically different plants

Indole
A natural plant chemical responsible for the rotten smell of some plants (for example, *Rosa foetida*) and the cloying sweet scent of others (lilies and jonquils)

Inorganic
A man-made chemical compound (one that does not contain carbon); inorganic fertilizer is produced artificially or refined from naturally occurring chemicals

Insecticide
A chemical used to kill insects

Irrigation
A general term used for the application of water

Lateral
A side shoot arising from an axillary bud

Layering
A propagation technique whereby roots are formed on a stem before it is detached from the parent plant

Leaching
The loss of nutrients by washing them through the soil

Leader
The main dominant shoot or stem of the plant (usually the terminal shoot)

Leaf
The main lateral organ of a green plant

Leaf mold
A compostlike substance formed from partially decomposed leaves

Leaflet
One of the small segments of a compound leaf

Lime
An alkaline substance formed from calcium

Loam
A soil comprising equal proportions of clay, sand, and silt

Loppers
Long-handled pruning shears used for pruning thick branches

Marginal plant
A plant that prefers to grow in damp soil conditions or partially submerged in water

Medium
(see *compost*)

Monoecious
Plants that carry both male and female flowers on the same plant

Mowing
Cutting down lawn grass to a required height

Mulch
A layer of material applied to cover the soil

Multirow system
A method of growing plants close together to regulate their overall size (also to control weeds)

Mutation
A plant change or variation occurring by chance, often referred to as a "sport"

Naturalize
To establish bulbs or other plants in grass so that they appear to have occurred there naturally

Nutrients
The minerals (fertilizers) used to feed plants

Olfactory
Related to the sense of smell

Organic
Materials derived from decomposed animal or plant remains

Outdoor storage
A method of storing produce outside but with some protection; for example, a potato clamp

Oxygenator
An aquatic plant that releases oxygen into the water

Pan
a) A shallow terra-cotta dish used for growing plants
b) A compacted layer of soil that impedes drainage and root penetration into the soil

Peat
Decayed sphagnum mosses, or rushes and sedges

Perennial
Strictly any plant that has a life cycle of more than three years

Pesticide
The generic name for chemicals used to control pests, diseases, and weeds

pH
A measure of acidity and alkalinity in a soil

Photosynthesis
The production of the compounds needed for plant growth by the synthesis of chlorophyll, light energy, carbon dioxide, and water

Pinching out
The removal (usually with finger and thumb) of the growing point of a shoot to encourage the development of lateral shoots

Plunging
A method of inserting plants into their growing site without removing the container from around their rootball

Potting on
Transferring a plant to a larger container

Potting up
Transferring young plants or seedlings from the seed bed/tray to a larger container

Propagation
Techniques used to multiply the number of plants

Propagator
a) A structure in which plants are propagated
b) A person who propagates plants

Protoplasm
A complex substance regarded as the physical basis of life (it can spontaneously move and reproduce), and which forms the living matter of all plant cells and tissues

Pruning
The practice of cutting plants to improve their growth or train them to grow in a certain way

Raised bed system
A system of growing plants in beds of soil above the surrounding soil level

Rambler
A vigorous trailing plant with a scrambling habit

Rhizome
A specialized underground stem that lies horizontally in the soil

Root
The underground support system of a plant

Rootball
The combined root system and surrounding soil/compost of a plant

Rootballed
Plants that have been dug up with the roots enclosed in a block of soil, which is held in place with burlap sacking or a similar material

Root pruning
The cutting of live plant roots to control the vigor of a plant

Rooting
The production of roots, usually from cuttings

Rootstock
The root system onto which a cultivar is budded or grafted

Runner
A stem that grows horizontally close to the ground, such as strawberries

Sap
The juice or "blood" of a plant

Scale
A modified leaf of a bulb used for propagation

Scarification
A method of damaging the seed coat to encourage germination

Scion
The propagation material taken from a cultivar or variety to be used for budding or grafting

Seed
A cellular structure produced by flowering plants that contains a dormant embryo capable of developing into an adult plant

Seed head
Any fruit that contains ripe seeds

Shoot
A branch, stem, or twig

Shrub
A woody-stemmed plant

Side shoot
A stem arising from a branch, stem, or twig

Spur
A short fruit- or flower-bearing branch

Stem
The main shoot of a tree

Stopping
Cutting out the growing point of a shoot to encourage the development of lateral shoots

Storage
A method of keeping plants in an environment that delays ripening and decay

Stratification
The storage of seed in cold/warm conditions to overcome dormancy

Sublateral
A side shoot arising from an axillary bud of a lateral shoot

Subsoil
The layers of soil beneath the topsoil

Sucker
A shoot arising from below ground level

Tannin
An astringent vegetable compound

Tap root
The large main root of a plant

Tender
A plant that is killed or damaged by low temperatures (below 50°F) and frost damage

Tendril
A thin, twining, stemlike structure used by some climbing plants to support themselves

Terminal bud
The uppermost bud in the growing point of a stem (also known as the *apical bud*)

Thatch
A layer of dead organic matter on the soil surface in a lawn

Thinning
The removal of branches to improve the quality of those remaining

Tip prune
Cutting back the growing point of a shoot to encourage the development of lateral shoots

Top dressing
An application of fertilizer or bulky organic matter added to the soil surface and often incorporated around the base of the plant

Topiary
The practice of trimming plants into formal shapes and patterns

Training
The practice of making plants grow into a particular shape or pattern

Transplanting
Moving plants from one growing area to another in order to provide them with more growing room

Tree
A woody perennial plant usually consisting of a clear stem or trunk and a framework or head of branches

Trunk
The main stem of a mature tree

Tuber
A root or stem modified to form a storage organ

Tying down
A method of using string ties for training shoots into a horizontal position

Union (graft union)
The point where a cultivar is grafted onto a rootstock

Variegated
Plant parts (usually leaves) marked with a blotched, irregular pattern of colors such as gold or silver on a base color of green

Vegetative growth
Nonflowering stem growth

Virus
A debilitating organism that lives inside the plant (there is no cure)

Volatile oil
An oil that evaporates easily; highly volatile plant oils (lavender) evaporate more quickly and provide a milder scent than plant oils with low volatility (patchouli, cedar), which evaporate more slowly

Waterlogging
A condition in soil where all of the air spaces are filled (saturated) with water and oxygen is excluded

Whorl
The arrangement of three or more leaves, buds, or shoots arising from the same level

Wilt
The partial collapse of a plant due to water loss or root damage

Windrock
The loosening of a plant's roots by the wind

INDEX

ACKNOWLEDGMENTS

The authors would like to thank Janis Wales, Alice, Alistair, Con, Gary and Mark from the 'Gardening Which' gardens at Capel Manor College, Middlesex. Julie Ryan and the staff at Capel Manor, particularly, Ian, Carl, Peter and Terry. Craig and the staff at Frensham Garden Center, Frensham, Surrey. Photographers Andrea Jones and Mark Winwood. Fiona and Linda at Limelight Management. Iain MacGregor, Anna Osborn and Anna Cheifetz from Murdoch Books. Chris and Nick Bradley for being so patient when we were busy.
Andrea Jones would like to thank all the gardeners and garden owners that helped her research and select plants for the photography of this book in the UK, Europe and USA. Special thanks to Peter Gregory for his continual support and assistance.

CREDITS

Photographs courtesy of The Alhambra, Granada, Spain (p.90, 142); David Austin Roses, Wolverhampton (p.42, 84, 117 left, 189 right); Brightstone and District Horticultural Society, Chelsea flower show 2001 (p.38); Andreas Bruun, Køge, Denmark (p.68); Chanticleer Gardens, Philadelphia, PA, USA (p.46); Crûg Farm Plants, Caernarfon, North Wales (p.48, 164, 180 right); Alex Dingwall-Main, Luberon Valley, France (p.49); Peter and Catherine Erskine, Cambo Gardens, Kingsbarns, Fife, Scotland (p.39, 40–41, 45, 74, 155 left, 188 right); Fleur Trouvé (front cover, p. 67 top right, 81, 124, 149); Glamis Castle, Scotland (p.7, 37); Eva and Roland Gustavsson, Sweden (p.67 right, 69 right); Heronswood Nursery, Kingston, WA, USA (p.75 center); Keukenhof Gardens, Lisse, Holland (p.50, 54); The Marchioness of Salisbury, Hatfield house, Hertfordshire (p.8, 16, 151 right); Mr and Mrs T.K. Marshall, Hunts Court, North Nibley, Gloucestershire (p.189 left); National Trust for Scotland, Crathes Castle, Banchory, Scotland (p.108); Natural Driftwood Sculptures, Bournemouth (p.9, 188 left); Norfolk Lavender Farm, Heacham (p.24); El Novillero, Napa Valley, CA, USA (p.118 center, 120 center); Royal Botanic Gardens, Kew (p. 86, 95 and assorted plant portraits); RHS Gardens Wisley, Surrey (p.149 right and assorted plant portraits); St Andrews Botanic Gardens, Fife, Scotland (p.109, 186 right); Westonbirt Arboretum, (p.111 right, 147 center); Major M.T.N.H. Wills, Miserdon Park Gardens, Stroud, Gloucestershire (p.92, 126, 146 center).

Laurel Glen Publishing
An imprint of the Advantage Publishers Group
5880 Oberlin Drive, San Diego, CA 92121-4794
www.laurelglenbooks.com

ISBN 1-57145-928-6

Library of Congress Cataloging-in-Publication Data available upon request.

Color separation by Colourscan, Singapore
Printed by C&C Offset Printing Co., China

1 2 3 4 5   07 06 05 04 03

Managing Editor Anna Cheifetz

Project Editor Michelle Pickering

Design Concept & Design Manager Sarah Rock

Plant portraits & garden photography Andrea Jones

Practical photography Mark Winwood

CEO Robert Oerton

Publisher Catie Ziller

Production Manager Lucy Byrne